The Spirit Whispers

Listening to Your Inner Voice

Dorothy K. Ederer O.P.

NEW PRIORY PRESS

EXPLORING THE DOMINICAN VISION

Dedication

I dedicate this book to my wonderful parents,
Ann and Bernard Ederer,
who have always been my greatest supporters
and dearest, most faithful friends.

I dedicate this book as well to my family:
Carol and Bob, Bernard and Judy,
Father John, Jeanne, Julie, and Gerri and Joe.
Their love and support has been unwavering
through happy and difficult times.

I also dedicate this book to my nieces and nephews
and their spouses: Colleen and Rob, Jenny and Martin,
Cheri and Larry, John Patrick and Shannon, David and Jenny,
Eugene and Nikki, and Eddie and Judi;
and to my grandnieces and grandnephews: Helena, Katlyn,
Kayleigh and Hannah, Bradney, RJ and Jacob.

Table of Contents

———— • ————

"Difficulties come when we don't pay attention to life's whisper. Life always whispers to you first, but if you ignore the whisper, sooner or later you will get a scream."

Oprah Winfrey

———— • ————

Foreword

At times, all of us have heard a voice deep within urging us to think twice or beckoning us to go forward with confidence. When we were in doubt of a given situation, we usually chose the kindest option or one that rang true to our best self. And when we were not sure about how much of ourselves to give, we opted to err on the side of generosity. We listened to that whisper.

Feeling the urge to do a kindness for someone else does not flow from what others might think. Peace flows from making something good happen and doing what is right. Just listen and follow that little voice inside you. Remember your experiences help you make wise choices and give you the confidence to act on what you know is right. Authenticity is always the best choice.

The following true stories are examples of what can happen to people when they hear that whispering voice within and respond with integrity and authenticity. As you read these stories, you will realize that these whisperings are not unique or rare. Instead, it is often the way God's Spirit touches the lives of each of us. Sometimes it may be that God is nudging us into a different direction for our lives or has some special work for us to do. Or perhaps he just wants to let us know that he is thinking of us in a very special way. This can happen when we come to the point in our lives where we realize that the most important part of praying is not in talking up a storm, but just being quiet and listening. God has so much to share with us.

Joseph F. Girzone
Author of the *Joshua* books

Acknowledgments

I would not have completed this manuscript without the encouragement and support of Fr. Andy McAlpin, my Dominican brother, who encouraged me to finish writing this book. Thanks also to Fr. Albert Judy, who got this manuscript ready to print. A special thanks goes to Kelly Sandula-Gruner for the exquisite cover design.

I especially want to thank my dear friends Jan Grabinski and Jean Shane for their expertise in proofreading this book. Their dedication has been such a gift in my life!

A special thanks to Fr. Joseph F. Girzone whose continual support and encouragement have been priceless.

Introduction

The following true stories witness how the Spirit works in our lives. They are living proof of what happens when we open our hearts and listen to the voice within. Each of us hears something different. However, we need to be open and willing to respond.

I chose the title, *The Spirit Whispers,* because of my mom's great devotion to the Holy Spirit. She peacefully listened and followed her inner voice. She encouraged us all to let the Spirit guide us in our lives. Our family used to tease her, dubbing her the "Bird Lady," because of her great devotion to the Holy Spirit. The first story will help you understand the reason for the title.

The first part of the book is compiled of stories or events I personally experienced. The second part of this book includes stories from family and friends.

As you read these stories, you will realize that they are not unique; rather it is often the way God's Spirit touches the lives of each of us. Hopefully, the following stories will help you see how the Spirit is working in your life, as you listen with your heart.

Here is a picture of me with the "Carrier Pigeon,"
but I will always call it "MY DOVE."

Whisper One: I Called It My Dove

We all stood praying at my mom's bedside before she died. We knew we were going to miss her terribly. Before she breathed her last breath, we asked, "When you get to heaven send us some birds so we know you are with God." She looked up at all of us and smiled. As we finished the rosary, we noticed she had died peacefully.

That evening I stayed at my sister Jeanne's house. The following morning she came running into my bedroom. "Dort, listen to those birds chirping outside." I jumped out of bed and we went to the window. Out in the yard were a number of birds singing happily in the early morning sunrise. Jeanne and I hugged each other and through our tears, cried, "Mom's in heaven; Mom's in heaven! Now she and Dad are together again!"

After my dad's death, I would see a double rainbow in the sky every year on his birthday. The year after my mom died I wondered if my dad would continue to send me rainbows on his birthday or if Mom would take over and send birds.

It was my dad's birthday. Before Mass that morning, Fr. Joe commented, "Well, now that your mom is gone, I don't think you will get any rainbows; from now on she will send you birds." Fr. Joe enjoyed teasing me a lot.

After Mass, I looked out the window and to my surprise I saw what looked like a white dove in the rose garden.

"Look Fr. Joe! There is a white dove in the rose garden!" Rushing to the window he said, "That's not a dove, it's a carrier pigeon; look at the ring on its leg."

I replied, "Well, it looked like a dove to me."

"Have you ever seen them up here before?" I questioned Fr. Joe.

"Never!" he answered.

After breakfast, we went to get the mail. The carrier pigeon was still there.

About two-thirty that afternoon, Chris, the gardener's assistant, called to me, "Sr. Dorothy, come over and look at this dove or carrier pigeon in the rose garden! It is weird; it won't fly away."

I replied, "Isn't it beautiful? Watch, it will follow me!" The bird followed me as I walked around the house, which was about 500 feet or more, and back to the rose garden. Chris stood there in amazement and said, "I've never seen anything like this; it acts like it knows you."

"Chris, I want to share with you a family secret. You see we always called my mom, "The Bird Lady" because of her great devotion to the Holy Spirit and when she died, we asked her to send us a bird so we would know she was with God."

"I keep thinking maybe...and then I remembered Fr. Joe mentioned one day that our loved ones have a way of letting us know that they are thinking of us. They tell us through unmistakable symbols. I believe this is Mom's way of telling me she is with God, and that she is always near."

Chris just smiled and went back to work in the yard. The dove stayed all week. I finally got a picture of me holding the dove [carrier pigeon]. [Fr. Joe told me that a real dove would not allow anyone to hold it, but a carrier pigeon would.] It flew away Saturday morning after our retreat and never returned.

The following Monday morning, Fr. Joe called me on the phone and said, "Look out your window; you won't believe it! Maybe your dad didn't forget you!" There, arched across the blue sky, was the most beautiful rainbow. I ran out to take a better look. Fr. Joe came out with his camera. I raised both arms and said, "Dad, I love you!"

Jokingly, Fr. Joe quickly observed, "But that's not a double rainbow; I thought you said your dad always sends you two, I only see one."

"Oh be real! It's a rainbow and I know my dad loves me; right, Dad?" I heard a whisper... and then I turned and looked back up to the sky. A double rainbow had appeared.

I will never forget the look on Fr. Joe's face. Laughing, I said, "That will teach you to mess with my dad." Blushing, Father Joe took a picture of the double rainbow which I treasure.

We believe that our loved ones are always with us in spirit. Just as I believe my mom sent me the birds to let me know she was with God, I also believe that God places a rainbow in each of our lives, offering us a covenant of friendship as we respond to God's love.

The Spirit Whispered: Remember I am with you in every situation. I have not disappointed you and will continue to guide you. I show my love for you in the simplest situations. Keep your heart open and trust me.

Prayer: Divine Spirit, you are there to assure me of your love. No matter how frightened I become, you do not disappoint me.

———— • ————

"None of us will ever accomplish anything excellent or commanding except when one listens to this whisper which is heard by that one person alone."

Thomas Carlyle

Whisper Two: The Spirit Guided Me

During my beginning years as a Dominican Sister, we were told by our superiors where we would minister; after ten years, we were allowed to pick our new placements. That was exciting for me. I could now find my own job! I remember being in Chesaning, Michigan; it was that time of the year when we discerned where God may be calling us next. One morning after prayer, around 7:30, I left the chapel still singing our closing song, "Here I am Lord, is it I Lord, I have heard you calling in the night."

I jokingly commented to the sisters, "Well, God will just have to call me and tell me where I am to go next." They all laughed with me.

It was only seconds later when the phone rang. Everyone looked at me; one of the sisters said, "Well, Dort, you better answer it!"

I picked up the phone, "Our Lady of Perpetual Help." The voice at the other end asked, "Is Sr. Dorothy there?" The look on my face told the sisters volumes. I looked at Sr. Adriana and said, "I think it's God." She giggled.

It was Fr. John Grathwohl from Kalamazoo, Michigan. He asked me if I would consider working in Campus Ministry. Still in shock, I said, "Well, I've never done that before. Don't I have to have a Masters in Counseling?"

He said, "Let me ask you one question; do you like children?" I said, "Oh yes, I love children!"

Fr. John then stated, "You can have all the degrees in the world, but if you don't love children you won't be a good campus minister."

I went for the interview, was offered the job and accepted the position. During my 13 years there, I took classes at Loyola University in Chicago, Illinois, to get a Masters in Pastoral Studies.

I also introduced the students to *Joshua*, a book written by Fr. Joe Girzone. The students, who had been reading his book, wanted to meet him. So I invited him to come to Kalamazoo. Over 2,000 people attended his presentation; we had to move the event to the Chenery Auditorium because our church wasn't large enough to accommodate such a turnout. His book made a powerful impact not only on the students but also on the University president who had tried to order religion off campus until he was given the book, **_Joshua_**.

After Fr. Joe's talk, he asked me to come and work with him in New York for the Joshua Foundation. I informed him that I had a contract for two more years.

He seriously said, "Well, break it."

"I don't break contracts."

He went to the pastor who wouldn't budge. "She would be perfect for that job, but I am retiring in two years; you can take her then."

Two years passed and one evening around 10:00 the phone rang. I hesitatingly picked it up; the person on the other end said, "Your two years are up; come and work with me."

Startled, I responded, "What? I don't think my community will let me go all the way to New York."

"Couldn't you ask?"

The next day I talked to my community and they replied, "Dort, this is your dream, to go around the world, telling others about Jesus; go with our blessings."

After praying, I decided I would accept the challenge. I found myself doing things I would never have done if I had not accepted this invitation. I gave talks all over the United States as well as in China, India and Switzerland. I would never have written a book except Fr. Joe's agent, Peter Ginsberg, asked me to write one. I published a number of books while working with Fr. Joe.

Several years later, I found out that my mom had bone cancer. They told me she had two months or less to live. I was stunned! I flew home and two and a half weeks later she went home to God.

A few years later my sister found out that she had cancer and my brother had open heart surgery, plus my niece was getting married.

I talked to God and said, "If you think I should be near my family, then you will have to find me a ministry close to them; I don't have time to look."

A couple weeks after that, I received a phone call from someone in Ann Arbor, Michigan, telling me about an opening in campus ministry. I was invited to come for an interview.

Other phone calls came for jobs in Michigan and in Indiana. After my visit to University of Michigan and my talk with Fr. Tom Firestone and Fr. Tom McClain, I felt called there. Fr. Firestone told me, "Do what you need to do to make this ministry what you think it should be. We need someone to help with retreats and other things." From all that Fr. Firestone and Fr. McClain said, I knew this was where I was supposed to be. I accepted the position. I was thrilled to be near my family.

Eight years later, I was reading my daily devotional, **_Jesus Calling_** by Sarah Young. The prayer that morning was, "I have plans for you that you can't imagine, plans for you to prosper. I will take you by the hand and lead you; just trust in me."

I prayed out loud, "God, I love working in campus ministry. I have been at Western Michigan University and the University of Michigan but not Michigan State. The pastor, Fr. Mark Inglot, had asked me three times, years ago, to come and work at St. John's at Michigan State University. He certainly will not ask me again."

I prayed, "If this is your will, then you will have to place these thoughts in Fr. Mark's mind, because apparently you have placed them in mine."

As I entered the student center that Monday morning to go to my office, there stood Fr. Mark Inglot, I was shocked! I felt paralyzed for a moment. He was with two of his friends, Judith Cardenas and Bernie Rochon. Frightened I said, "Why are you here?"

He just replied, "I thought you would be happy to see me." I waved my hands over my face and smiled and then said, "Welcome, Fr. Mark, great to see you."

Judith said, "Yes, she would be perfect." I said, "Perfect for what?" Her husband responded, "Yes, you should get her. Didn't he tell you we own a moving van company and can move you."

"What?" I exclaimed. I laughed; then said to Fr. Mark, "Do you have ten minutes?"

"Yes! Of course!"

We went into my office and I told him about my prayer that morning. His response was, "Well, listen to God this time. I really need you to help me. You can write your own job description and are free to create and do what you need to do."

I told him, "That is the same thing that Fr. John Grathwohl told me when I first went into campus ministry."

His comment touched me deeply. What a gift! I said to Fr. Mark, "You mean I am free to create and do what needs to be done? This is like another dream come true!"

I told him, "I am still in shock, I can't believe this is all for real. I want to pray about this. I will let you know when I return from spring break."

When I returned from spring break I called and gave him my answer, "Yes!

Now I am the Director of Campus Ministry at St. John Student Parish at Michigan State University and loving it! The parishioners and the students have been so welcoming. I love ministering with them!

The Spirit Whispered: Trust in me. I am here to help you become all that I want you to be. Thanks for listening and being open. I will never disappoint you. Just turn to me and you will be happy and at peace.

Prayer: Divine Spirit, you continue to lead me on new paths. Help me always to be open to you. Listening to you and what you have planned is the most amazing adventure.

———— ◆ ————

"We need to make a conscious decision to allow the Spirit to help us hear God's word and have the courage to live it day to day."

Brendan McGuire

———— ◆ ————

Whisper Three: Yes, I Believe in God

Dennis Lu, a professor at the State University of New York, invited Fr. Joseph Girzone and me to China to help plan an exchange program for college students. I convinced Fr. Joe that it would be an exciting experience for us. As authors, we both were very interested in this trip as we wanted to better understand the attitude of the Chinese toward Christians.

When we arrived in China, we met Xinan Zhu, who was the Director of the Commission of Education in the district of Quilin; she was also a Confucius expert. Xinan was in charge of 300,000 students in the city of Guilin, which included students from kindergarten age through the teachers' colleges and graduate schools.

One evening at dinner, Xinan said, "Dorothy, can you come and teach my women your philosophy of life?"

I smiled and whispered to Fr. Joe, "I wonder how many nuns I could bring back from here?" He just smiled.

I replied graciously, "I already have a job, but thanks for thinking of me."

After three days, we left to visit other universities. As I was leaving, Xinan stopped me in the stairway and asked, "Do you think I will ever see you again?"

I said, "Nothing is impossible with God!"

Every year, in Washington, DC, Congress holds the National Prayer Breakfast inviting ambassadors and diplomats from all over the world. Fr. Joe arranged for Congress to invite Xinan, as he believed she could be a help in establishing a relationship with the Chinese people. Xinan came and stayed with us in Alexandria, Virginia. Fr. Joe also introduced her to some of the churches in Washington.

The three of us attended the National Prayer Breakfast; Xinan had the opportunity to meet spiritual leaders and government officials from almost 200 different countries. Many of them were Muslim, Buddhist or Shintoists. One of the things that impressed Xinan the most was that the prayer breakfast was centered around Jesus, whose teachings encouraged love of others and forgiveness of enemies.

Three days later when she was leaving, she asked me, "What can I bring back to my students?"

I said, "Teach them to love and to forgive each other. If you can teach them that, you will have a beautiful school year!"

She said, "Great! That sounds like a good idea!"

At the end of that school year, she received a call from the top Communist officials in Beijing inviting her to receive an award for all she had accomplished in the past year.

What impressed the Communist officials the most was the radical change in the students' behavior throughout that school district, as previously it had been rampant with drug abuse and crime. That year, the officials were shocked when they realized that there had not been one incident of crime or drug abuse throughout that vast school district. Because of this accomplishment, Xinan was presented with a very prestigious national award that listed her as one of the 100 most important, influential women in China. They arranged for her to speak in important places throughout the country. This news spread throughout all of China including Hong Kong.

Meanwhile, the local Communist officials in Guilin were upset because she had changed the curriculum in the schools, and was teaching things in the schools that were forbidden. Other incidents were also reported to these officials about decisions she had made in delicate situations. For example: One day a student, in one of the classes, brought up the subject of the violence that had taken place in Tiananmen Square. The professor was upset with some of the things that the student said and reported him to Xinan.

The professor said, "Xinan, I think he is trying to start a riot."

Xinan asked, "Was he telling the truth?"

"That is not important," the professor said.

Xinan then said, "I **cannot** punish a child for telling the truth."

Then a different professor reported that a couple of girls went to church.

Xinan asked, "How do I punish children for what they believe?"

The professor said, "But they believe in God."

Xinan looked down. Then the professor asked her, "Do you believe in God?"

Xinan paused for a moment and looked the professor straight in the eye and replied, **"Yes."**

The next day she was fired from her position and put under house arrest for six months. She was interrogated continuously, and her house and phone were being monitored. Her husband, who was a doctor, was not allowed to return home and live with Xinan. She was totally isolated. One day her husband secretly contacted her and told her that she must leave the country as soon as possible as he had learned that the local officials had decided to have her executed.

Xinan had been secretly contacting Fr. Joe through friends and they gave her the information she needed to get out of China. Fr. Joe advised her to leave the house and go to Beijing, where she could get a visa to go to Canada. Fr. Joe also told her that he would do whatever he could to arrange for her to come to the United States. When she arrived in Canada, she stayed with her son.

Meanwhile Fr. Joe was able to talk with the people from the National Prayer Breakfast in Washington, D.C. and they agreed to hire

Xinan, if she could get into the country. The officials tried to make arrangements for Xinan to come from Canada, but had no success because she was not coming from her home country. Fr. Joe then called the American Embassy in Toronto and talked to the official in charge; he explained to her the horrible situation Xinan was in.

The official invited Xinan to the Embassy and gave her a visa to visit the United States for six months and advised her to seek political asylum. Finally, arrangements were successfully made for her to work in Washington, D.C., obtain political asylum, and receive a green card from the Federal Government to work in the United States.

Xinan was able to visit Fr. Joe and me at Joshua House, and we spent many wonderful days together. Her son, from Toronto, was also able to to visit us.

While she was with us, Xinan developed a deeper understanding of Jesus and the Catholic faith, which brought back memories of her mother taking her to Mass on Sunday mornings as a child.

One day, as I was driving her down the driveway, she said to me, "There are three people who live here on the mountain."

I said, "No, there are only two of us."

"No, there are three: You, God and Fr. Joe."

That was the second time she said she had experienced the presence of God in Joshua house.

She grew to love Jesus, the scriptures and talked about becoming a Catholic. One day while reading the bible, she came across the passage, "If you can't forgive your brother and sister from your heart, then I cannot forgive you."

She called me and said, "I don't think I can be a Catholic."

"Why?" I asked.

"I don't think I can ever forgive what the Communists did to my family."

"Why Xinan, what did they do that you can't forgive them?"

"They drove us into the street, took over our palace, killed my mom who was pregnant, then eventually killed my dad, and then my one brother."

My heart sank. I felt so sorry for her and could not imagine what she must have gone through. Fr. Joe and I explained to her that, "Forgiveness is a process. It takes time. We may not always forget, but as long as we don't want to get revenge, in time we eventually will be healed."

After a year of study and prayer, she finally decided that she wanted to be a Catholic. Fr. Joe baptized her and we both felt honored to be her Godparents. I would often pray with Xinan and hoped that eventually she could forgive those who killed her family and destroyed her home.

A few years later, she came to one of our retreats. After my talk on forgiveness, she stood up and said, "I think now I can call myself a real Catholic!"

I looked at her and before I could ask why, she said, "Because I have forgiven them from my heart!"

She told her story to all those on the retreat and expressed her sorrow. The entire group was in tears. What a sacramental moment that was for all of us!

The Spirit Whispered: Learn to forgive, because lack of forgiveness will cause more damage to you than to the other person. Holding in anger and resentment will eventually destroy your spirit and can even affect your health.

Prayer: Divine Spirit, help me to be a forgiving person. Heal me of hurtful memories and help me to understand why people are hateful. Help me not to be offended so easily. Forgive me for the times that I have hurt others, as well as the times I have been impatient or critical.

Whisper Four: The Flight Is Coming In!

It was a cold winter day in March when the students at Western Michigan University in Kalamazoo were getting ready for a speaker to arrive from New York. They had prepared all week for his arrival.

His plane was to arrive that afternoon and his talk was scheduled that evening at eight o'clock. It came across the news that, due to weather conditions, the airport was being closed and there would be no more flights that day.

I told our pastor that I was going out to the airport anyway to try and pick up our speaker. When I arrived at the airport, I found a few other people there with hope in their hearts for a change in the weather so that planes would be allowed to land.

I went up to the counter and asked the attendant if she thought that this particular flight would arrive since it was later in the day. She said: "No, ma'am, I am sorry but not one flight has arrived today and we don't expect any this evening."

I said, "It has to come in because there are so many people waiting for our speaker and I don't have time to drive to Detroit and back." (Kalamazoo is at least two hours from Detroit airport.)

She said, "I am awful sorry, ma'am, but there will absolutely be no more flights today."

I replied, "Well, I am going to pray that this flight does arrive."

She smiled and said, "Good luck!"

I saw a young man waiting for his girlfriend's arrival and asked him if he would pray with me that the flight could land. He smiled and said, "Sure, but you can say the prayer and I will sit here with you as you pray."

I prayed that if it was God's will, we needed this flight to land. So many people (about two thousand) were depending on this speaker, Fr. Joseph F. Girzone, to share the message of Jesus.

In the meantime, unbeknownst to us, the plane was circling the airport and the pilot said, "We will circle one more time and if they don't give us the okay to land, we will have to go to Detroit."

About five minutes later, the pilot said, "We just got the okay to land; I can't believe this. Someone up there must really be on your side!"

All the people coming off the airplane were smiling.

A young lady ran to her boyfriend, "You won't believe what we just went through; our flight circled the airport three times and we finally received clearance so we could land! It was like a miracle!"

The young man replied, "Well, that lady over there was praying that it would." She glanced at me with a puzzled look and I just smiled. All the people were sharing their excitement about their arrival as they came off the plane.

Fr. Joe finally came off the plane; he slowly walked up to me and explained what had happened. I smiled and told him that we were praying while they were circling the airport. He laughed, "You are something else, Dorothy; you Dominicans certainly believe in the power of prayer!"

"We sure do!"

The Spirit Whispered: Have faith in me, I will always be there for you, I will never forget you or leave you!

Prayer: Divine Spirit, our prayers are always heard, sometimes we may not like the answers, but our strong faith will help us see that whatever the answer is, we know it will be for our good.

Whisper Five: No Worries, It's Not a Problem!

It was a rainy day in June when my train ride to Chicago lasted much longer than planned. The conductor told us that we could not go any faster than fifteen miles an hour because of the flooding from the rain. This would make my trip to Chicago seven and a half hours long instead of four hours. I was scheduled to arrive in Chicago at 12:15 p.m., but with this delay we would not arrive until 3:30 or later. I asked the conductor where their next stop would be. He told me that they would have to stop in Indiana. I decided to call my friend, Monique, and share the situation with her.

She said, "No worries, I will come and pick you up in Indiana. I am only forty-five minutes away." I was deeply touched by her generosity.

The phone rang a few minutes later and she said, "If there are others who would like a ride, I can take about four more people besides you."

I overheard the man behind me trying to find a way to get into the city for an important meeting, so I introduced myself and asked him if he wanted to ride with us. He was so appreciative. As I got off the train, I saw two young women trying to find a taxi. I went over and extended the invitation for them to join us. They were very grateful and informed me that they were helping a young couple with a baby who had to get to Chicago and wondered if they could also come along. I asked them, "How old is the child?"

"A year and a half," was the reply.

I said, "Let me call Monique and ask her if she has a car seat for the child." I couldn't believe it when she said she had one in her car. She arrived about fifteen minutes later and we all started piling into the car. After fifteen minutes of manipulating the luggage, we were finally settled and ready to head into the city. There were eight people in the SUV with ten pieces of luggage, three pillows, and four purses. We were so packed in her car that we weren't sure if we would be able to get out. There wasn't room for one more thing.

As we started our one hour drive into the city, Monique asked if everyone would give their name and tell her something about themselves. Our trip was delightful. We had quite an interesting group. The two women were planning on going to college next year: one to the University of Michigan, where I was a campus minister at the Catholic parish, and the other to the University of Wisconsin. The young man sitting next to them worked for Homeland Security and the young couple was from India. We laughed and shared quite a bit about our lives.

When we finally arrived in Chicago, we carefully got out of the car and said our goodbyes. One young woman offered Monique some money but she graciously refused and said, "No, pay it forward; now you can do something for someone in need."

Everyone was deeply touched by her kindness and generosity. While we knew that we might never see each other again, I knew for sure that I would be seeing the young woman who planned to attend the University of Michigan and my dear friend Monique, whose friendship is priceless.

The Spirit Whispered: Never miss an opportunity to help others in need.

Prayer Divine Spirit, everyone wants to make a difference of some sort in this world. Monique, with her generous spirit, reached out, and not only touched one life, she touched all of us in her car. Help us always to be concerned about others. May we never be so consumed with ourselves that we miss an opportunity to be Jesus to others.

Whisper Six: I Can Start Now To Forgive My Dad

It was August when I arrived in Altamont, New York, for my new job working for the Joshua Foundation. The construction workers were just finishing the home they were building for me.

Anxious and excited to start my work, I asked Fr. Joe, "When are we going to start our work?"

He said, "Relax, Dorothy, God will send people or they will call us when it is time."

By the second week I was getting concerned that maybe I would not be traveling, giving talks and retreats. Joe told me one morning after Mass, "God knows what he is doing, Dorothy; he is just giving you some time to relax and when it is time, we will receive phone calls and requests to do our work. It won't be long and you will be so busy you will wish you had some time to rest. Trust me on this."

In the meantime, I visited with the workmen. They shared their struggles and concerns with me. It made me feel needed and I felt like I was at least doing what I was called there to do. Then I heard a whisper—*it will come soon ...just wait.*

At the end of the month it all happened. We started getting phone calls to give talks and retreats. I was so excited. Our first speaking engagement was at a place in the South.

The priest who invited us didn't tell us that he didn't get permission from the bishop for us to speak until we arrived. He said, "I am so sorry Sister Dorothy but you won't be able to speak today, and Fr. Joe, I don't know what to say. I could get in trouble for having you here."

Fr. Joe said, "We are a team, if she can't speak then I guess I can't either."

The priest was a nervous wreck. First of all the church was packed and secondly, a few people told him they were going to start a petition against Fr. Joe. Their plan was to get up and walk out in the middle of Fr. Joe's talk to make a statement. Finally the priest said, "Well, since you are both here let's go for it, and I guess Sr. Dorothy can talk after you, Fr. Joe."

I sat in front behind Fr. Joe watching the congregation and waiting to see what would happen. About halfway through his talk, a couple of women got up and moved to the back row of the church, but they never left.

Then it was my turn to give my talk on forgiveness. I noticed a little girl in the front row smiling at me as I walked up to the podium, I smiled back and said to myself: "I know she must be here for a reason. Jesus, help my talk on forgiveness to help at least one person." I silently prayed, "Be with me Holy Spirit and help me say what I need to say to these people; may forgiveness touch the heart of at least one person tonight."

I delivered my talk and afterward walked out to where people were lined up for our book signing. The little girl who was sitting in the front row, came running up to me and threw her arms around me and started to cry: "Please help me to forgive my Daddy." My heart went out to her and I held her as she cried.

Her mother walked up to us and said to her daughter, "Come on, let's go." She looked at me and said, "She'll be fine."

The little girl turned to her mom and said, "Mom, can we ask her to pray with me so that I can forgive Daddy?"

I turned to the mother and asked if that would be all right with her. She looked again at her daughter who said, "Oh, Mommy, please!"

The mother said "okay" and backed away while her daughter and I went off to the side and prayed. After we finished our prayer, the daughter came running to her mom and said, "Mom, I feel so much better, I think I can start forgiving Daddy."

The mother looked at me and started to cry. She said, "I was with a group of women tonight who were supposed to get up and walk out on the talks but my daughter would not let me, so we stayed. I guess now I know why we could not leave." I reached out and gave her a hug and then her daughter joined me and the three of us hugged right there in the vestibule of the church. They both thanked me and left with tears in their eyes and a smile on their faces.

The women, who had moved to the back of the church in the middle of Fr. Joe's talk, stayed the entire evening. A few of their friends said, "We are glad we didn't leave. We needed to hear what you two had to say tonight, thanks!" I gave them hugs and thanked God for the blessings of the event.

The Spirit Whispered: The children will lead them. Listen to the children. I rejoice in children's insight and persistence.

Prayer: Divine Spirit, sometimes we judge people by what we hear about them. However, when we get to know them, we begin to see their goodness and sincerity; then all the rumors and untrue things just melt away. Help me learn not to judge others on hearsay, instead help me get to know them for who they really are!

———— • ————

"We all have a story to tell,
whether we whisper or yell."

Author Unknown

———— • ————

Whisper Seven: We Need Light!

It was a lovely day in June. The flowers were in bloom and the sun shone brightly on the mountain. Jim and Luanne were visiting from Michigan. They wanted to climb the mountain before leaving the next morning. Since it was about 8:00 p.m. when we started up the mountain, we decided to take flashlights to help us find our way back.

As we approached the top of the mountain, we stopped and marveled at the beauties of creation and all the twinkling lights across the valley. Suddenly, we heard men's voices. I walked over and asked, "What are you guys doing up here?"

"We came to enjoy this beautiful view. Isn't God great?"

"Yes, God is awesome! But how did you get up here?" I asked them.

"We drove our truck up the old dirt road."

"Is it a pickup truck?"

"Yes!"

"Does it have a cover on the back?"

"No, it is open."

"How would you like to give us a ride down the mountain? It's so dark now and we are afraid of getting lost or falling on our way down, especially through the woods."

"Sure, we'd be glad to help you out but first we need to borrow your flashlight to help us find our truck."

Thrilled that we didn't have to venture down the mountain in the dark, we helped guide them down the path until we found the road where they had parked their truck.

We all hopped in the back. As we rode through the woods down the bumpy lane, we started wondering what we may have gotten ourselves into.

Luanne asked me, "Do you know these guys, Dort?"

"No, I just met them."

"What! You must be kidding me. You mean you don't know these guys? How do you know they won't hurt us? They could be taking us deeper into the woods instead of taking us home. What did you get us into? This is crazy!"

"Oh, don't worry, they seemed like two nice guys. After all they did talk about how wonderful God is, so they can't be too bad. Anyway, we are all here together; what can they do to all three of us? A little voice inside me said, "You'll be fine."

It was so dark that all we could see ahead of us were the headlights on the road. The trip through the woods seemed like it was taking longer than I thought it should.

When we finally reached the highway, we asked them to drop us off at the end of Leesome Lane, which is about a half a mile from our driveway. They insisted on taking us all the way home.

When the truck arrived at the driveway, Joshua Lane, I shouted, "This is fine right here, it is just a short walk to the top!"

"How far is it to the top?" they yelled back.

"It's only a half a mile. We can walk." The driver insisted that he take us all the way home. "My mom always taught me to be a gentleman and take people right to their door," he said.

Now we became nervous. We were at their mercy.

Just as we arrived at the house, Fr. Joe came rushing out to see who was driving the truck. He was annoyed with me and went over to meet the men.

As we jumped out of the truck giggling, Fr. Joe introduced himself to the men and invited them in for dessert. He had prepared a special dessert for us and was worried when we were an hour and a half late.

The two men graciously accepted the invitation.

As we stood around eating and chatting, Fr. Joe invited the two men to watch a video he wanted us to see. Of course, they were delighted. We all watched the video. It was after one o'clock before they decided to leave.

Before they left, they asked Fr. Joe a lot of questions about his home. Fr. Joe explained that this place was used for retreats and he gave both the young men a copy of *Joshua.* One of the young men was from Brazil. He recognized the title and spoke up, "My grand-mother loves this book and even sends copies to her friends. She is coming from Brazil to visit me tomorrow. I can't wait to tell her about my evening!"

"You are welcome to bring her here tomorrow, if she wants to come. Give us a call and let us know."

The next day, the young man from Brazil called and asked if he could bring his grandmother up to meet Fr. Joe. They arrived an hour later. We had refreshments and sat and chatted for over an hour. The woman, whose husband was a senator in Brazil, told us she had been praying that her grandson would find God. She was so happy he had met us.

When they were leaving, the young man said to me, "You need to know this, last night YOU were the *light* that led me to my truck as well as to Jesus. I didn't sleep last night because I had to finish reading *Joshua*. I have been searching for a Jesus that makes sense for a long time. I want to follow this Jesus! Thank you so much, Sr. Dorothy."

The Spirit Whispered: You never know when I am going to ask you to be a light for others.

Prayer: Divine Spirit, light the flame of trust in our hearts. May we never doubt that you are always there to help us. Continue to guide us toward the light of truth and honesty. When all seems hopeless, you always bring us back to you.

Whisper Eight: Don't Give Up!

Friends from the Ukraine told us that every time they prayed the "Our Father" and came to the words: *"Yours is the Kingdom, the Power and the Glory,"* they were reminded of what happened to them when they wanted to build a church.

In the Ukraine, a group of people who had been gathering and praying together for years, wanted to build a church. They needed $30,000 to build one. They asked an organization for some money. They were told if they could earn $10,000, the organization would give them $20,000 to build their church. The community accepted the challenge and raised $10,000. So they received the remaining $20,000 necessary to build their church.

The community then went to the government to purchase some land. The government sold them swampland, but even that did not stop them. They took their wheelbarrows and hauled dirt to fill the area. It took six months before they could build on it. They wanted lumber for their church, but the only way they could get lumber was to cut down their own trees. They decided to ask the government for bricks. They were told if the community agreed to tear down a silo, then they could use those bricks. So they tore down the silo. In the process of tearing it down, they found a bullet shell in between a few bricks, and inside the bullet shell was a piece of paper. The message on the piece of paper read:

> *"These bricks were purchased to build a house to worship God, but they were confiscated by the government to build a silo. May it please the Lord that these bricks will one day be used to build a house to his Glory."*

The Spirit Whispered: Never give up on your dreams!

Prayer: Divine Spirit, may we always remember that it is your kingdom we are building, not ours. By building God's kingdom, we can make a difference in our world. We can make the world a better place—a safe place—one that is built on love and trust. Help us to build your kingdom.

Whisper Nine: An Atheist Who Is Closer to God Than He Realized

While working for the Joshua Foundation in New York, Fr. Joe Girzone and I were invited by Anna Bell and Bill Brue to speak in Switzerland. We would be speaking to diplomats as well as some of the wealthiest people in Switzerland, many of whom were atheists.

The evening before our talk, they had a dinner and invited a few of their closest friends. At the dinner, Jan, the Swedish ambassador, said to Fr. Joe, "I have a very difficult time believing in a God who allows all the evil that happens in the world today."

I looked down at the other end of table where Fr. Joe was sitting and could see he was getting upset. I put my finger up to my lips signaling to Fr. Joe not to say anything as we were their guests.

Then Jan continued saying, "I have an even more difficult time understanding why a person would dedicate their whole life to a God like that?"

I looked around and everyone's eyes were cast down toward their soup. Then I saw the look on Fr. Joe's face. I knew that these were fighting words and there was no way he was going to keep quiet. Fr. Joe's response was, "You know I believe in God and pray every day, and I think I am a good person. However, I think if you were God and people did things you didn't approve of, you would zap their free will. You see, Jan, once God gave us a free will, he can't violate it. He has more respect for our free will than you Jan. Obviously, you don't believe in free will as much as God does."

"Jan, suppose you were a billionaire and you came across a tribe in the middle of the jungle who had all sorts of medical and physical needs. You wanted to help them out but you could not stay. You found some intelligent people, people you thought you could trust. You gave them a fortune to take care of all the needs of those poor people. Then you left."

Now those intelligent people said, "Why should we waste our money on the others, we are wealthy now. Let's keep the money to ourselves, then we will have the power and all that we need or want."

"Should those poor victims blame you for not helping them, when you gave all that money to these people to take care of them? Could they blame you? That would be illogical. It is not any more logical than you who are involved in the United Nations and associate with the wealthiest people in world. You have all the resources to help the poor and yet you never get your act together enough to help them. It doesn't make sense that you blame God for the mess the world is in when you do nothing."

"Jan, I am a priest and I think about God a lot and say nice things. I even pray a lot, but I have a funny feeling that I spend nowhere near the time thinking about God that you do."

"Jan, you think about God day and night. God is always on your mind. I think you are a lot closer to God than you realize."

"Father, you are something else! I came to this dinner tonight so I would not have to go to your talk. But I will be at your talk tomorrow for sure."

We went into the living room after the meal and the ambassador asked me, "Dorothy, what do you do for a living?"

I proceeded to tell him who I was and what I did. He shook his head and said, "You people amaze me. I can't believe what you do with your lives."

The next day a huge crowd gathered. I looked to see if our friend Jan was there. Sure enough, I saw him walk in and sit down.

After singing a couple songs, we gave our talk. After our talk, we had refreshments. I went down to talk to the people and as Fr. Joe was walking, someone grabbed his arm. It was Jan, he was crying. He looked at Fr. Joe and said, "Thank you! Thank you so much."

Then he said, "Where is that Sister? I want to see her before I leave."

He came over to me, reached out and gave me a hug. I was shocked but thrilled! That evening was an experience I will never forget.

It is challenging and exciting to see how the Spirit works in the lives of people.

The Spirit Whispered: Never give up on what you believe. I will work in the hearts of all people and help them to be open to change. Trust me and continue doing what I have called you to do.

Prayer: Divine Spirit, help me to care for those less fortunate. Never let me be so self absorbed that I don't see the needs of those around me.

---·•·---

"It's impossible." said Pride.
"It's risky." said Experience.
'It's pointless." said Reason.
"Give it a try."
Whispered the Heart.

Author Unknown

---·•·---

Whisper Ten: I Believe in Miracles!

I was invited to give a talk to a group of women in New York. After my talk, I was approached by six women who asked me to pray with them.

They said, "Sister, we want you to pray for a miracle."

I stopped and said, "What did you want me to do?"

They said, "We need you to pray with us so this woman is cured of cancer. If you pray with us, we believe she will be cured of cancer. She has three children at home and they desperately need her. Please help us."

My response was, "I will pray with you, but please don't think that because I am praying with you that a miracle will happen. I know God says it is our faith that can bring about healing, but honestly you scared me. If it is God's will, she will be healed."

The women were persistent. I smiled and said, half kidding, "Well, there are seven of us, each of us can represent a sacrament."

"Which one are you?" asked a woman.

"Well, in the convent when our class shrank down to seven, we named ourselves the seven sacraments. I was given the name, Confirmation, because I kept affirming the other sisters that they had a vocation. I didn't want to be the only one left. I think we need to call upon the Holy Spirit to help us here."

I didn't realize until we started praying that these women belonged to a Charismatic Prayer group. Talk about powerful prayers! It was beautiful.

While praying, I felt warmth I never felt before. In fact, my hands and arms were getting hot, like someone plugged me into a heater. I was afraid to look around and kept my head down.

After about fifteen minutes, we ended our prayer. The two women, holding my hands on both sides said, "Well you certainly have hot hands!"

I said, "Mine? No it was your hands that were hot."

Then everyone shared that they felt the same thing. It was frightening for me because this was the first time I had experienced anything like this.

Before we parted, I asked them, "Please let me know how the appointment with the doctor turns out, okay?"

I gave them my phone number, signed a few books, packed up my belongings and headed home.

On the drive home I was talking to God and asked God to help me understand what just took place.

When I got home, I called Fr. Joe to tell him about what had happened. He said, "Don't worry about it. It's all in God's hands."

I thought about the woman who had cancer and prayed that God would do what was needed for her family.

The next day about 3:00 in the afternoon, I received a phone call. One of the women in the group said, "Sr. Dorothy, you won't believe this. She doesn't have to have surgery! It's a miracle!"

I was shocked. "Tell me what happened."

"Well, she went in to see her doctor and told him she didn't feel the lump anymore."

He said, "This can't be."

She asked him to examine her and take an x-ray before doing the surgery.

He respected her wishes and examined her. Then he took an x-ray. He found nothing. He called in a couple other doctors for a consultation. They agreed there wasn't any lump or any sign of cancer.

Her doctor said, "I don't understand. Three weeks ago there was a lump, a large mass but this test revealed to us that it is gone! I am not sure what happened here." He just shook his head and said, "I guess you can go home."

The woman said, "See Sister, God does listen. Now let's have a party to celebrate this wonderful miracle!"

Words can't express how this experience affected my prayer life. God is continually working miracles. We have to have faith. We have to be aware and open.

A few years later, my brother John had poor circulation in his legs and a blood clot in one leg. One leg was beginning to turn black. While visiting him in the hospital, his doctor told me, "If his leg isn't better by the morning, we may have to amputate."

I asked my brother if I could pray with him over his leg. I asked him to forgive anyone he may not be at peace with so that God could heal him.

While praying, my hands became very hot.

Then I remembered the time I prayed with the group of women in New York and what happened. I asked God for another miracle. We finished our prayer and I left.

The next morning I received a call from my brother. I noticed that the call was from his home. I said, "John, are you home?" As only a brother would say, "Well, isn't this my home phone? Then, yes, I am home."

I asked, "What happened?"

He said, "When the doctor came in to check me this morning, he took one look at my leg and was shocked. He could not believe the improvement. He decided I could go home." Then he continued, "It was amazing, this is the first time in months I am able to get into my cowboy boots. All the swelling is gone!"

God continues to heal us and help us in times of need.

The Spirit Whispered: Miracles happen every day. You need to pay attention. I will let you experience things you never imagined. Trust me at all times.

Prayer: Divine Spirit, you continue to work miracles and heal people. Help us to be aware of the miracles that happen every day. Continue to heal all that needs healing in us as we continue to trust in you.

Whisper Eleven: What Makes You Write Books?

Early one morning, I received a phone call from Stacy Spitler, Director of Communications for the Grand Rapids Dominicans, who asked me what made me write books.

My response was, "I was asked to. Every time I write a book it is because I believe the Spirit is inviting me to write."

"Are you kidding me?"

"No, I am not. In 1998 while I was in Old Town, Virginia taking some time to relax and write some talks, I received a phone call. It was Peter Ginsberg, who is Fr. Joseph F. Girzone's agent. He asked me what I was doing. I told him I was writing a talk. He proceeded to ask me what it was about. I shared a little bit with him."

He then said, "Dorothy, let's put it in a book."

I said to Peter, "I am not a writer. Fr. Joe is the writer."

He said, "Well, we will see about that. I think your talk would make a good book. "

"No, Peter, you are Fr. Joe's agent, I don't think this is a good idea."

He laughed and said, "We'll see. I will call Doubleday and get back to you."

Still in shock, I thought there was no way he would convince Doubleday to publish a book from someone who had never written one before.

Three days later, Peter called to inform me that he had a contract for me with Doubleday. He requested an introduction and a couple chapters done in a couple weeks. I turned to Fr. Joe and said, "I am not a writer, I can't do this."

He replied, "Yes you can, do you realize how unusual this is? No one is asked to write a book. I believe that God wants you to do this and you will."

So, I began writing the book. Three months later I received a phone call from my sister Jeanne. She told me that Mom was diagnosed with bone cancer and had been given a life expectancy of two and a half weeks to two months. I was in shock. I shared this with Fr. Joe and told him that I wouldn't be able to finish the book. He said, "Yes you will, God wants you to write it! I will call Doubleday and ask that they give you some extra time because of your mom.

Doubleday was gracious enough to give me an extension. I went home and two and a half weeks later my mom went home to God.

I asked the Holy Spirit to help me finish the book because I had trouble focusing and my mind was not really into it. Not only did I manage to finish it on time, but I was honored with an award for the "Best First Time Author."

Two years later a friend of mine, who was a blind, pro golfer passed away. I called his wife to offer my condolences. She shared with me what happened. After first losing his sight, then his leg, and having four strokes—all about eight years apart—he was in the hospital. While his wife and children were there, he pulled off his oxygen mask and looked up at his family. She said that the gray film lifted from his eyes and they were as blue as the sky. He saw them all for the first time in 28 years.

I said, "Jan that is a miracle, I have to tell the world about this. His story will be chapter one in my new book."

When I shared this story with Peter, my agent, he told me that I definitely had to write this book. A year later, Doubleday published, **The Golfer's Day with the Master.**

Four years later, I was called to work as a campus minister at the University of Michigan. Because my book was no longer selling as well as when I was working for the Joshua Foundation in New York,

Doubleday gave me back my rights. Peter told me that he believed the book would still sell if I found a Catholic publisher. Since I didn't know who to contact, I just put the thought aside and continued my ministry.

The following summer Chris Tremblay, a former student from WMU, encouraged me to teach at the Chautauqua Institution in New York. At first, I didn't want to go as I got my summers off and felt I needed some time off. Chris insisted that I at least apply. With the hundreds of applications to teach that the Institution received, I figured I didn't stand a chance, but I still completed the application. I couldn't believe I was accepted. Next, I had to find a place to stay and Chris told me about the Catholic House in Chautauqua. Because space was so limited, you had to enter a lottery and pray that your name would be picked. My name was drawn.

My first morning at the Catholic House as I came downstairs, I ran into a priest. He looked familiar to me and then we both recognized each other. It was Fr. Mike Kerrigan, a campus minister. He told me he was the publisher for Paulist Press. I looked at him in disbelief. I asked him, "What is your favorite area for publishing?"

He said, "Sports."

I replied, "You won't believe this, my agent told me to find a Catholic publisher to publish my golf book."

Surprised he said, "I don't have any books on golf, send it to me." He then handed me his business card.

After I returned to my ministry a few weeks later, I thought about what had happened. I honestly thought that Fr. Mike was just being kind and didn't do anything about it.

Six months later, I woke up at three o'clock in the morning. I thought I heard the Spirit shouting, "I send you a publisher who wants to publish your golf book and you think he is being nice. Call him and get this done."

It haunted me for a couple days especially since I could not find his business card. Frustrated, I went to work, opened my top desk drawer and there was his card. I knew the Spirit wanted me to call Fr. Mike. I called him and we arranged for the book to be published. They titled it: **A Golfer's Prayer Book**.

Four years later, I asked Fr. Andy McAlpin, a Dominican, to give a talk at our spring retreat for Michigan State University students. When he arrived, we started sharing what had happened in the last year. He told me his religious order had just opened a publishing company and he asked me if I would like to write a book. I told him I didn't have time. He said, "Well then, you better make time because I will get it published if you write it."

I told him I had started a couple of books but hadn't been able to discipline myself enough to finish them. He assured me that once I got him the book, he could get it back to me in six weeks. I found that encouraging, since it takes most publishers a year. I finished the book I started. It is called: **Spiritual Nourishment**.

When God wants me to do something, it is very difficult for me to ignore. I hear the whispers and yes, sometimes even the shouts; however, deep in my heart I know I will respond as he is my God.

The Spirit Whispered: Listen to my promptings. I always want what is best for you. I have plans for you and your ministry. I will help you to be the woman religious I want you to be.

Prayer: Divine Spirit, I am so grateful for your continual support and love. You have always been my guide. Help me to listen and respond.

The following **Whispers** were submitted by family and friends.

Whisper Twelve: Let Me Walk with You

It was over 25 years ago when I listened to that inner voice.

I was born and raised Catholic and even attended parochial schools in Grand Rapids, Michigan during the 50s. I was well tuned into what it was to be a "good Catholic." I went to Mass each morning, tried my best to observe the Ten Commandments and church doctrine. I was a product of my parents' generation, I learned what the Church expected of me and tried to follow the template provided.

What was my relationship with God? There wasn't one, really. Everything I did on that front was more avoidance of the punishment I assumed was in place for not being a "good Catholic." I was far from angelic as a young boy but with the magic of Catholicism, I was able to receive absolution through the confessional. Once again, all was right with the world.

My relationship with God was based on avoiding punishment rather than an intimate friendship, something that at that time I didn't even realize was possible. In fact, if asked, I would have thought that kind of relationship to be unthinkable. I couldn't imagine someone as unworthy as me being a friend with God?

Based on conversations I have had with many of my friends over the years (Catholics and non-Catholics alike), my perspective was a pretty common one at the time. This perspective carried on into college, married life and through starting a family. I never really strayed from the Church but I was mostly going through the motions. Something was missing...I needed more from my faith life. The fact that I realized this suggests that something greater than I was nudging me...but where and what? I was one of the lucky ones. Having worked my entire career at Western Michigan University, my family was blessed as we attended St. Thomas More Student Parish.

The atmosphere there was/is joyful, compassionate, and contagious. But still, I hadn't moved anywhere on my spiritual journey. Clearly, the Spirit needed to bump up the "whisper" to a healthy shove.

Enter Sr. Dorothy Ederer. While I knew who she was, I didn't know her on a personal level. But there she was. Every month or so, I would hear her promoting this book, *Joshua*, by Fr. Joseph Girzone. Probably six months went by before I said to myself, "If she is this passionate about the message in this book, I should probably check it out." While Sr. Dorothy wasn't "whispering," the comment I made to myself was clearly driven by the Spirit, as I wasn't into reading spiritual works. So, I purchased the book. I could not put it down. I was highlighting and making notes all through the book. Nothing I had ever read in my life made me feel so good and yet so guilty about being a Christian. That probably doesn't make sense, so let me explain.

Fr. Joe's book showed me a compassionate, caring, forgiving, and loving God I had never met before; a God who is quite comfortable meeting you right where you are. I had never considered that God would love me absolutely without conditions, and would do so whether or not I loved him. This just seemed crazy. The Prodigal Son comes to mind here. This realization was an absolute game changer. But to be honest, it just seemed too good to be true. So, since Sr. Dorothy was the one who convinced me to buy the *Joshua* book, I introduced myself and asked to meet with her to discuss all these confused and conflicted feelings. She agreed to meet and we spent several hours going through all my questions and notes. At the end of that meeting, I was absolutely walking three feet off the ground. The time I spent with her was the beginning of an incredible friendship with not only Sr. Dorothy, but later with Fr. Joe as well.

Since that day, my life and relationship with my God has been forever changed and I am eternally grateful to both Sr. Dorothy and Fr. Joe for what they have given me.

The Spirit Whispered: *Come as you are, let me walk with you....* I have no preconditions; I'm not only there when you call or when you're perfect. I know that you need me, especially when you're lost and hurting and I will always be there for you....*come as you are; let me walk with you.*

Prayer: Divine Spirit, thank you for always loving me unconditionally. I know that there is nothing I can do to deserve the grace you freely give me. I am grateful for your generous and forgiving love. Help me to appreciate the special gift I have with you, and help me to witness that love to others who may cross my path...in your holy name.

Lowell P. Rinker, Retired CFO
Western Michigan University
Kalamazoo, MI

———— ◆ ————

"*Whisper a wish to a butterfly and it will fly up to heaven and make it come true.*"

Author Unknown

———— ◆ ————

Whisper Thirteen: No, God, Absolutely Not

I was teaching fourth grade religious education classes one evening a week. I would go in early to prepare for classes. I guess I was spending a little too much time at the parish as our deacon approached me one afternoon and suggested I consider becoming a deacon. He thought I had the requisite qualities. My response was, "No, not me!" He chuckled and didn't press the matter. I recall thinking I was not qualified. I am just an ordinary guy, not holy enough or intelligent enough to be a minister in the Church.

A few weeks passed and a fellow parishioner who was in deacon formation, approached me and suggested I consider the diaconate. Again, without hesitation, my reply was, "No, thank you!" I thought to myself, these guys really do not know me. Yes, I was becoming more active in the parish. However I was very comfortable being a lay volunteer, nothing more.

A couple of weeks later the parish custodian approached me and suggested I consider the diaconate. Our custodian is an ordinary guy but very spiritual. I would see him at Mass and it appeared he had a very devout, intimate relationship with the Lord. Well, I didn't say no; instead I shook my head side to side and nervously walked away. What was going on? I felt like a conspiracy was at work. Obviously, these three guys had gotten together to convince me I should be a deacon. I didn't even think of including the Holy Spirit as a coconspirator.

Quite frankly, I was scared to death. The idea of standing up in front of a church full of people and preaching was frightening. There is no way I could do that. Just the thought of it made me nauseous. During this period, a number of the Sunday readings involved "call" stories. I began praying more intently for courage, understanding, and knowledge. The more I prayed the more at peace I felt. I went back to the deacon and got more information about the program. He said it was the Holy Spirit that prompted him to approach me. He recognized the Holy Spirit growing in me. He suggested I speak with the pastor. I agreed thinking there was no way the pastor would go along with this crazy idea.

Wrong again! The pastor said he had had his eye on me. I asked if he was sure it was me. He was positive. He suggested I start the diocesan ministry formation program and see where it might lead. I enrolled in the program. It contained twelve undergraduate theology courses. The entire time I thought that if God really wanted this to happen, he would continue to nourish me with the Holy Spirit. I did well in ministry formation, eventually applied and was accepted into the deacon formation program. After a long process, I was ordained.

I am completing my fifth year as a deacon; it has been an experience beyond my wildest dreams. Each time before I get up to proclaim God's Word or I am about to do a formal ministry visit, I call upon the Holy Spirit to set aside my ego and give me courage to be God's spokesperson. The Holy Spirit provides the extra support I need and the event always becomes something more than I could have done alone.

The Spirit Whispered: I reside in you and I am here to strengthen and empower you. All you need to do is believe and trust in me.

Prayer: Divine Spirit, help me to set aside my false self, my ego, and allow you to shine through me. Give me courage to be the person you have called me to be and not hold back!

Gary Prise, Deacon
St. Mary Magdalene
Brighton, MI

Whisper Fourteen: Love in Fire and Ice

God, as many of us now know, comes to us in many unexpected ways. The story of my life, while perhaps unique, is certainly not all that uncommon because many of us have experienced "the God of surprises."

My earliest years were quite common but nevertheless unique. I was the only child of a university professor father and an artist mother. We were regular Catholics, a standard Catholic family, faithfully attending Sunday Mass every week. Raised in Ann Arbor, Michigan, I attended University of Michigan High School and then the University of Michigan, majoring in Business Administration.

In my junior year of college, I met Judy. It was life-changing. While many don't believe in "love at first sight," I do. I fell, and I mean totally fell, in love with her and wanted to live the rest of my life with her.

In my senior year, I was given the opportunity to attend University of Michigan Law School and so, in the summer of 1955, I began attending classes in law school. Looking back, that was a fateful decision, fateful because it meant that marriage would be postponed. That, of course, changed Judy's expectations. I realize now that I had not taken her hopes into account, something that even now, nearly sixty years later, gives me moments of regret. Without going into the sad details, my relationship with Judy ended when she shut the door. There was no closure and that was that. I never knew her reasons for breaking off all contact with me; I only have conjectures.

The day after Judy closed the door, I rose early in the morning and headed over to St. Mary Student Chapel for 7:00 a.m. Mass. During the night, a soft rain along with freezing temperatures had coated everything in ice. The tree limbs glittered with light reflected from the streetlights along the campus walkways. It was an epiphany of sorts, coincidently enough on January 6, 1956, the Feast of the Epiphany. It was then that I became aware of God speaking his words of love in my heart telling me, "Charlie, your world may be covered in ice but within that ice there is fire and love." Those words are as fresh in my heart today as they were back then, sixty-seven years ago!

In the days that followed, I attended Mass daily. As time went by, I began reading books written by Thomas Merton, the most important of them being **The Seven Story Mountain.** My prayer life intensified. I found companionship with a fellow freshman in law school, a very spiritual young man named Jim who was a graduate of the University of Notre Dame.

Interestingly enough, Jim and three other of my law school colleagues eventually entered seminaries to study for the priesthood. Two of them were ordained priests. One dropped out of the seminary before ordination. Of the three of us who were ordained, two have passed away.

The loss of Judy threw me into a deep depression, as you might imagine. Thoughts of quitting law school and just "giving up" beset me. My heart was crushed. Nevertheless, I plodded on.

In May of 1956, my father was diagnosed with very late stage lung cancer, and by early August he was dead.

"Why, I asked God, did you do this to me? If you are such a good and loving God, why do you allow suffering, particularly in the lives of those who love you?" Similar questions and heavy thoughts came my way. At some point, I noticed that I was questioning God in an accusatory way. Eventually, with the gentle movements and whispers of the Spirit within me, I began to ask those questions in an inquisitive way.

I finished my courses in law school whereupon I took the bar exam. I went to work in the Trust Department of one of the largest banks in the country, a Chicago bank which handled the trusts and estates of very wealthy clients.

My social life was dismal. No one was able to capture my heart the way Judy had. Unbeknownst to me, the Holy Spirit was at work shaping me to eventually be a priest: a priest who would be sensitive and caring to those with broken hearts, to those who feel as if God had abandoned them and to those who knew suffering, loss, and pain in their hollowed out hearts.

Thoughts of becoming a priest came more frequently and it was not long before I began discussing my inclinations with a priest stationed at Chicago's Holy Name Cathedral Parish. The time came when I tendered my resignation to my employer.

My last day with the bank was in June of 1960. My colleagues gave me a goodbye party in a bar in Chicago's Loop district. During that party, a female stripper appeared and my "friends" began to snicker and make "remarks." It struck me that I no longer represented just me. I represented Jesus Christ, the Church, and the priesthood. So, in the midst of the mocking, I got up and departed. My companions followed me outside. I said my goodbyes, crossed the street and turned to give them a final wave. It was there that the Holy Spirit really made his presence known. Above their heads was the name of the bar we had just vacated. Its name was *The Crossroads*!

The Spirit Whispered: I will continue to surprise you and help you do that which will bring you peace and happiness. Trust in me. Listen to me closely. Love will be your guide.

Prayer: Divine Spirit, my companion and friend. Help me to realize your presence deep within me. In my moments of darkness, fill me with your Light. Give me wisdom and understanding when I am beset by confusion, when my mind is filled with this world's clutter. In my weaknesses, give me strength and courage during those times when I am moved by the temptations and voices of this world. In the midst of its busyness, let me listen to your whispers so that I might follow your paths as I make my journey through the life you have given me.

Fr. Charles Irvin
Catholic Priest
Diocese of Lansing, MI

———— ◆ ————

"God's Holy Spirit within us changes our hearts to be humble, kind and compassionate, as well to be fierce to protect the innocent, and wise to make good decisions. God is passionate."

Tess Calomino

———— ◆ ————

Whisper Fifteen: The Spirit Came In The Mail

I became a principal in 1998. After being a classroom teacher since 1980, it was a great career move. However, somewhere in the back of my mind I truly felt that God was also whispering to me that after 18 years, it was time for us to make a physical move. This thought kept coming back to me over the next two years.

In the early months of 2000, something extremely interesting happened one day. I came home from school and opened the mail. One envelope in particular caught my attention. I recognized the handwriting. It was a letter from my father-in-law. Truthfully, I would have to say that this was the first time I had ever received a letter from him, even after being married to his daughter for 20 years.

I went into our bedroom, opened the envelope, and a small square ad from a newspaper fell out. It had been cut out of the *Western Catholic Reporter* monthly newspaper. The ad, from the Edmonton Catholic School District, was advertising for principals to apply to the district. My father-in-law had simply written, "Do what you need to do!"

I was stunned. How did my father-in-law know that I was thinking about making a change? I never spoke to him about looking for a new position, let alone moving to where he was living. We had been living 600 kilometers [360 miles] away from my wife's family for the past twenty years.

When my wife came home that evening, I said, "Look what your dad sent me today!"

We sat and talked about the ad. We came to the conclusion that, "It wouldn't hurt to apply, so go for it." So I did.

After filling out an extremely long application that involved getting ten colleagues to write their thoughts about me as a school principal, and after making a very long trip to Edmonton for an interview, I received a call and a letter indicating that I had been successful in my application.

I had one problem. We had just completed building a brand new school. I would essentially be completing the building of the school and moving away at the same time. It just didn't seem right to me. So I called Edmonton and spoke to an Assistant Superintendent of Human Resources. I told him how excited I was about coming to Edmonton, but that I was wondering if he would be willing to wait for one more year before I made the move. It was like I had released a pressure valve. He responded immediately by telling me that he would be very happy to accommodate my request given that they had also been experiencing some changes in the district and that a move for me to Edmonton in a year would be best for them as well.

One year later, my wife and I and our three daughters moved to Edmonton. I began my career as a principal at St. Gerard School in inner city Edmonton. It was amazing. I had suddenly moved from a Catholic school district of 11 schools to a school district with 88 schools.

It wasn't all about me either. In the ensuing years, my wife went from a classroom teacher to an assistant principal to principal of her school. This would never have happened in our previous location. As well, each of our three daughters met and married three fine gentlemen, and we now have four grandchildren. We have been truly blessed.

The Spirit Whispered: Put your complete trust in me and I will make sure everything works out as it should. Be not afraid and all will be well, because I am with you.

Prayer: Divine Spirit, you walk beside me and are the wind beneath my wings. I pray that I will seek your wisdom and guidance at every turn in my life. I thank you for the gift of life and I trust completely in your love.

Dan Friedt. Principal, Catholic Schools
Edmonton, Alberta, Canada

---•---

"Too often we underestimate the
power of a touch,
a smile, a kind word,
a listening ear, an honest
compliment
or the smallest act of caring,
all of which have the potential
to turn a life around."

Leo Buscaglia

---•---

Whisper Sixteen: The Spirit Finds Me

I know the Spirit is alive and well in my life because I am constantly experiencing moments in which "the Spirit finds me." What do I mean by that? It's my version of serendipity. Serendipity is defined by Merriam Webster as "luck that takes the form of finding valuable or pleasant things that are not looked for." However, I don't call it luck. I call it the Spirit working in my life. I share here four short vignettes which demonstrate how the Spirit has found me.

At a recent new student orientation at the university where I work, I randomly selected a family to greet and welcome to campus. As we were talking, the mom saw my nametag and said, "Oh my gosh! You are the person that we were told to talk to." They wanted to know about our Catholic campus ministry program and someone was aware that I was involved in the Catholic student parish affiliated with the university. So, I was able to share with them my experience and give them a referral and a contact person. Now, what are the chances, among the hundreds of students attending that orientation program that I would happen to pick that family? The Spirit finds me.

My current job found me. I was enjoying my position at another university when one of my former professors called to see if I was interested in considering a new job at my alma mater. I had previously worked at my alma mater, where I earned two degrees. It was a dream come true to return to where my college days started. This was a part of God's plan and I was to follow where I was being led. I had left 10 years previously never expecting to return. But this job found me, as I wasn't even looking for new employment. Now I received the honor of having the same impact that others who went before me had on me. I listened, prayed, and followed. The Spirit whispered.

In the spring of 2014, I ran into a prospective student and his family on campus as they were getting ready to take a campus tour. I engaged them in some friendly conversation as part of welcoming them to the campus and providing hospitality. After a few minutes, we learned that the student's mother had lived one street away from me in my hometown suburb near Detroit! Talk about a small world. Again, I had no plans to approach this family, but randomly encountered them on campus and we made this discovery. It was evident that this exchange brought comfort to this family and personalized a large university for them. You could call it divine intervention. They found me as I had not searched for them and was not even aware that they were coming for a campus visit. The Spirit whispered and united us at that moment.

My last example took place when I was finishing my doctoral dissertation. I attended a presentation by a colleague who worked in our library. She was presenting information regarding an online tool for publishing journals. The Spirit found me. I was inspired by the presentation, took the information I had learned and merged it with one of my professional hobbies: college access. Voila! The Journal of College Access was born. The Spirit found me! And thanks to my partnership with two colleagues, this idea became a reality.

The Spirit Whispered: Trust in me and let me guide you since I know you better than you know yourself. I will see that you are where you need to be.

Prayer: Divine Spirit, may we be open to how you guide us on life's path. Place us where we need to be to serve others and make a difference in their lives. Use us as your instrument.

Christopher W. Tremblay, Ed. D.
Associate Provost for Enrollment Management
Western Michigan University
Kalamazoo, MI

Whisper Seventeen: The People You Meet Impact Your Future

Several years ago, I coined the expression, "The people you meet impact your future." It was another way of saying, "It's not what you know, it's who you know." I firmly believe that the Holy Spirit presents many gifted individuals in our lives to impact us and our futures. We are so blest to be interpersonally connected to wonderful friends and family members. This story tells of the special women in my life and how they impacted me and how I pay tribute to them. These individuals are all gifts of the Holy Spirit.

The most influential woman in my life has been Sr. Dorothy Ederer, O.P. I had the good fortune of meeting Dorothy when I was a college student attending St. Thomas More Catholic Student Parish in Kalamazoo in the 1990s. She witnessed to me how you can be yourself, follow Jesus, and listen to the Holy Spirit. Twenty-three years after our initial meeting, our relationship has flourished. Sr. Dorothy opened the door to how God is at work in our lives. She is a living testament and has impacted the future of many college students through her day-to-day ministry as a campus minister. Dorothy nurtured my spiritual future. It has been enriched by her presence. I entered college never really knowing a Catholic sister and she entered my life and became a dear friend. You never know who God is going to introduce to you, now or in the future!

I would not be where I am today if it were not for two women in my professional life who actually departed their employment, which opened up doors for me. In 1998, my former supervisor, Diane, took a job elsewhere, which enabled me to receive a promotion at work. I was so excited about my new job. Unfortunately, her opportunity was not a good match, but I feel that God was at work in both of us and I'm still grateful to this day for having been led by the Holy Spirit. A similar experience happened again in 2010 when a colleague, Judy, took a job elsewhere. This enabled me to receive yet another promotion, this time at a different university. Again, that opportunity was not a perfect fit for Judy. Yet her vacancy gave me a gift. As I reflect on these experiences, both women heard the Spirit whisper, listened, yet sacrificed to my benefit. I will forever remember these experiences and will be indebted to their choices. Now, more than ever, I am conscious of where God leads me and how that benefits those individuals whom I leave behind. As some say, when one door closes, another door opens.

These three women enriched my future and opened many doors for me as the Spirit whispered to them.

The Spirit Whispered: Be open to the people who enter and exit your life.

Prayer: Divine Spirit, continue to send individuals into my life. I pray that I will remain open to every one of them and I trust that they're there for a reason, even though I may not know it now or later.

Christopher W. Tremblay, Ed. D.
Associate Provost for Enrollment Management
Western Michigan University
Kalamazoo, MI

Whisper Eighteen: One Step at a Time, Paris To Chartres

Life is a pilgrimage, a journey to our heavenly destination. Each step in our lives brings us closer to God, whether we are on the right path or we need to stop and rest, or we need to turn around and go another direction. Our path leads us to Resurrection.

The career part of my life's journey began with public and Catholic school employment, followed by 22 years working for the Michigan Department of Education. I retired and found myself busier than ever. Family elders and friends needed my assistance. I pitched in and found fulfillment in sharing my time and talents. I joined an athletic club and worked hard to maintain my health. I became a regular participant in retreats at Transformations Spirituality Center in Nazareth, Michigan. I loved retirement!

One of the retreats I attended in June of 2012, Sacred Threshold, was led by Paula D'Arcy. Paula shared many inspirational stories including one from her experience as the co-leader of a walking pilgrimage in France. It sounded like a crazy thing to do....walk over 50 miles in three days? However, in her story she described a middle-aged woman who had not trained for the journey, nor had she come prepared with the right walking clothes and shoes. Yet, with the help of the pilgrim group, she completed the walking pilgrimage. I was impressed.

Two months after the retreat, I was inspired to register for the pilgrimage. However, there was no room left on the roster. So, I asked to be placed on the waiting list. I decided this was a good sign. If God wanted me to experience this pilgrimage, a spot would open for me. I was also advised that the labyrinth in the Chartres Cathedral would not be available for us to walk during the time in Chartres. Again, I turned this over to the Holy Spirit praying, "If it is important for me to experience the labyrinth, please provide access to this ancient prayer space."

On January 10, 2013, the email announcing an opening arrived. I was absolutely thrilled and began training in earnest!

On April 29th, I departed for the pilgrimage, my first overseas adventure, traveling alone to meet up with 18 strangers. A friend advised, "Imagine yourself stepping through a portal and over the threshold into a powerful experience." Yes, it was that and more.

The air was filled with excitement as the group boarded the Paris subway car headed for the Notre Dame Cathedral. With packs on our backs and sturdy walking shoes on our feet, we were eager to begin our journey through the French countryside. The goal was to reach the Cathedral of Our Lady in Chartres by late afternoon the third day.

Day One was a glorious piece of cake. We walked eight miles from Notre Dame Cathedral in central Paris past the Sorbonne, to the Church of St. Jakob where we prayed for blessings on our journey. We made our way through the city streets, noticing the change in architecture and open spaces. The sidewalks provided easy passage. Our steps took us eight miles before we boarded a train and then a bus. By the time we reached our lodging, I knew I needed to lighten the backpack, a real lesson in determining what is essential for living!

Day Two was much more challenging. We had been walking along a rutted path for about a half hour when I fell flat. I was scared to death given a recent diagnosis of osteoporosis, but nothing was broken or even bruised. I thanked God that I was okay, dusted myself off, and continued with my companions. We walked ten miles through farm fields of bright yellow canola. After lunch, we walked about 30 minutes and took a break in a lovely grassy area. My calves started to cramp badly. So, my break was cut short to try anything and everything to alleviate the cramping. We had ten more miles to hike before we reached the hostel. I began to think I might not be able to complete the pilgrimage on foot. But, the Spirit whispered, "One step at a time, Jean, just take one step at a time." It felt like an old friend was encouraging me with those words. Often I was only able to take just one step at a time, stopping frequently. But each one step, added together, became the 19+ miles we walked the second day.

Day Three was really difficult and totally wonderful. Before setting off on the rural path, we each bought something to contribute to a picnic lunch since there would be no restaurants or public facilities to visit along the way. I really didn't want to carry one more item, but the delight of our community meal was a great tradeoff.

After lunch, the anticipation of reaching Chartres Cathedral was electric. Everyone was exhausted. One last break, and then, as we turned a corner we could see the spires of the cathedral in the distance...a two-mile distance...Yikes! I needed the Spirit's encouragement each step of those last two miles... "One step at a time, Jean, just one step at a time."

The blessings of the pilgrimage continued through our time in Chartres. Paula and our local guide, Gernot Candolini, provided spiritual and historical sessions. We attended Sunday Mass in the packed cathedral; visited the crypt; walked the exterior catwalk along the edges of the high roof; entered the attic space to view the amazing rafters; and were surprised to be granted an after-hours personal time in the Cathedral where we were able to pray the labyrinth in this amazing sacred space lit only by the fading daylight. The silent prayer while walking the labyrinth was an amazing time of grace and peace.

Upon my return to Michigan, I was faced, along with my brothers and sisters, with the decline of our aging parents.

My parents are the best! They raised three girls and four boys. Dad was a pharmacist and the owner and manager of an incredibly successful, service-oriented, neighborhood pharmacy/gift store. Mom was a parish newsletter editor and secretary. Each actively participated in community service activities including the hospital service league, Ladies Library Association, Rotary, Red Cross, Hospice, and a multitude of parish programs. Above all they are people of faith. They love God with all their hearts, souls, and minds and their lives reflect this love.

About five years ago, my parents began to ask for assistance with financial tasks such as balancing their checkbook. I was happy to help, driving the 80 miles to their home at least once a month to review statements and assist with decision-making.

As time progressed, the siblings began to share concerns about the parents' abilities to drive safely. We talked with Mom and Dad about our concerns, but they continued to drive.

In the summer of 2013, we had another conversation about driving and also asked if they would like to move to a one-story home to eliminate the use of stairs. They did not want to make a move and insisted yet again that they could continue to drive safely.

As my mom approached her 85th birthday and my dad his 93rd, they became more and more frail. All this time, my siblings and I were praying for the Spirit to guide us and our parents. Decisions were not going to be easy, no matter who had to make them.

Then, on October 5, 2013, my parents told us they wanted to move to Wyndham Apartments, an independent living building that is part of a continuum of care retirement community in their hometown. They said, "We've decided it is time to move to Wyndham." You could have knocked us over with a feather!

My parents were able to secure an apartment that met most of their stipulations. A moving date of November 21st was established.

Five days before the moving van was to arrive, my brother Rick announced that his house, that had been on the market for six months without any interest shown, had sold. He wondered if they could rent the folks' house for several months, until they found a house in their desired community, hopefully before the start of the 2014-2015 school year. Talk about an answer to prayer! The house would not have to sit empty all winter.

The timing was perfect! Our parents were able to relocate; we were able to prepare the house for Rick and his family; and Rick was able to move in, all before January 1st.

Through all these personal and family events, I truly believe the Spirit is with me always as an old trusted friend with great encouragement, "Trust me, Jean, one step at a time. Trust me!"

The Spirit Whispered: Trust ME. I am with you every step along the way.

Prayer: Holy Spirit, when I believe I can't take another step, help me to trust that you will guide me along life's path and give me the strength to take one step at a time.

Jean M. Shane, Retired Senior Policy Advisor
Michigan Department of Education
Mason, MI

"*Dreams are the whispers
your heart responds to.*"

Author Unknown

Whisper Nineteen: The Spirit Whispers Again and Again

As a single mom of young children, I was fortunate to serve as the Executive Director of the Michigan Chapter of the Cystic Fibrosis Foundation. Prior to this job, I was only making $7,500 a year teaching. My teacher's pay was hardly enough to live on as a single person, let alone as a single mom with three children. Therefore, I felt blessed to have a job where I loved my work, the people I worked with and was making enough to support my children. During my nine years, the foundation grew and the demands of my job increased. I was out of town a lot. My children were entering junior high and high school and I found trying to meet the demands of my family and my job exhausting. I didn't know what to do. My mom suggested that I pray to the Holy Spirit for guidance.

I prayed for months but I was still uncertain what to do. One night, driving back from an event on the other side of the state, I happened to listen to a program on the radio. They were discussing prayer. The message was simple: *Be specific when you pray. Ask for what your heart desires and then leave it to God to do what is best for you.*

As I pondered these words I thought: Is this possible? Does God want me to be specific when I ask in prayer? What do I think is best for me?

I turned off the radio and drove in silence for some time. Then I began to pray:

> *"God, I would like a job where I can work from my home. My children need me at home. I'd like a job where I can use my experience in education and business and still be able to serve my children and community. If possible, I'd love a job where I can travel and see the country. God, maybe I am being a little bold to ask for so much. However, you know what is best for me."*

Months went by and I forgot what I really prayed for that night. During a luncheon meeting regarding sponsorship for a major event, I shared the benefits of supporting the Cystic Fibrosis Foundation. After sharing both my experience and the Foundation's opportunities, I asked Dave, "Would you like to sponsor an event for us?"

He answered "No."

Surprised, I said "Really?" Since he was so interested, I was sure that he wanted to be a part of this worthwhile cause. I was disheartened. However, what he wanted was to hire me for one of his businesses. He thought I would be a great fit. His company provided educational materials and training for middle school students (I had taught grades 4-6). The job entailed asking businesses to sponsor a program (this is what I did in my current job) and then work with superintendents and teachers to implement the program in the schools. The job would require travel across the United States a couple days each month. My children's dad recently moved back in town and wanted time with the children which would give me the freedom to travel.

Dave asked, "Do you have enough space in your home for an office?"

"Yes, Dave, I do have an extra room for an office!" I was shocked! Dave was offering me exactly what I had asked God for in prayer. This new job would use my skills and experience. I could work out of my home and be with my children! I would also travel and see the country! I thought—*this is a miracle!* The Holy Spirit had whispered into Dave's ear everything that I had prayed for and I could hardly believe what I heard.

I have to admit, I was so afraid to leave the job that had offered me a stable and secure future. However, how could I doubt the involvement of the Spirit? The Spirit whispered: "God knows what is best for you. Trust me!" God knows the desire of our hearts!

After all the details were discussed, I wrote my resignation letter and faxed it to the Cystic Fibrosis Foundation. I called my immediate supervisor and informed her of my decision. She was shocked. She knew I loved my job! But I knew my family needed me more at this time. Then I received a call from the Vice President of the Foundation. He was surprised and asked me about my decision. I shared with him the reasons for my decision.

He asked me to take the weekend and consider a regional position, within the foundation, where I could work out of my home. He would call me on Monday to determine if this was a possible solution for both of us.

Meanwhile my brother warned me about leaving a job where I had served nine years as the Director. He said, "Be careful about accepting a position from a relatively new company. It can be risky!" I valued my brother's opinion because he owned several small businesses.

I was in a quandary. How could I ignore what seemed to be a divine response to my prayer? Was God now leading me in a different direction?

On Sunday morning I picked up my mother for church as I did every Sunday and shared with her my latest dilemma. "How do I know what God wants me to do?"

Mom, a strong believer in the power of the Holy Spirit, advised me in her usual manner, "Jeanne, ask the Holy Spirit. Listen carefully. The Holy Spirit will tell you." Mom was always so calm and certain that the answer would come if I would just ask and trust.

The Gospel that Sunday was one of my favorites. Jesus asks Peter, amid a storm, to step out of the boat and walk on water to him. Imagine how frightened we would be in this situation? What an act of faith! The priest began the homily:

"Like Peter, we may be asked to leave what is comfortable; God may want us to do something that we view un-reasonable; God may ask us to do what is frightening for us. Maybe God is asking you to step out of a boat. Maybe you need to step out of an abusive marriage. Maybe you need to leave a job that **you've been in for nine years...**"

What? Did he say nine years? I was so shook that I didn't hear the rest of his homily. Dumbfounded, I looked at my mom. She raised her eyebrows and hands and whispered, "You wanted an answer? Well, I think you got it!"

Yes, I took the new job. My second week, they sent me to an international conference in Cancun. The job was more than I had dreamed possible.

The Spirit whispered, "I am with you." In my case, I felt the Spirit blew me a kiss saying, "I love you!"

The Spirit Whispered: I am with you in every area of your life. Like the wind that blows and the fire that burns inside you, I will surround you with love. I am with you always and especially in your time of need. I know your needs before you speak them. I speak in your heart and in the hearts of others. Please listen to me.

Prayer: Divine Spirit, your love is powerful! You are ever present and move in our hearts and minds. You ask us to pray, to listen and then to follow where you lead us. You set us afire with courage and show us the way—no matter how frightening. Please show us the way.

Jeanne Murphy, Retired Marketing Director
Yeo & Yeo, P.C. CPAs
Saginaw, MI

Whisper Twenty: Sorrow Looks Back. Worry Looks Around. Faith Looks Up.

It was December of 1999. My husband and I were enjoying our new home on the lake having lived there just a year and a half. We loved our new home and all the fun things attached—boating, water skiing and just sitting on the deck overlooking the beautiful lake. In the winter we toured our surroundings on our snowmobile. Often, the kids came with their ice skates and sleds to enjoy the frozen lake. We had a wonderful life both in the summer and the winter. Life was good as we enjoyed our dream surroundings.

Then one morning my husband woke me up; he said he needed to go to the hospital as he was having chest pains. With much emotion, I drove him to Saginaw where he was admitted to the hospital. Within a few days he was scheduled for heart surgery. I was satisfied that he would be healed and we could get on with our dream life. The family gathered on the day of surgery and stayed together to hear good news. I kissed him before they wheeled him away, never dreaming I was kissing him goodbye. He died during heart surgery as our family stood by, overcome with tears of grief.

Thus began the most difficult time of my life. I was 19 when we were married. We had been married 41 years. I had never lived alone and knew I could not continue to live in the home that was meant for both of us. The days that followed were filled with tears and grief. Sundays seemed to be the hardest. One Sunday, filled with heartache, I started to drive with no destination in mind. I wanted to cry alone. As I drove, I came upon a subdivision on a small lake that my husband and I had once considered. The subdivision had mostly larger homes; they were big and beautiful. As I drove through the subdivision, there was a smaller ranch with a "For Sale" sign in the front yard. I felt this home calling out to me like I had never felt before. It was as if it was waiting for me.

I called my son who was a real estate broker. He set up an appointment and we toured the home which overlooked the lake. I knew without a doubt that I wanted this home. My son tried to counsel me and said, "Mom, it's too soon for you to make this decision, and you haven't even sold your home up north yet. But since you've never listened to me before, I'm sure you won't now."

My reply was, "I want this house, prepare the paperwork."

Soon after, I put my northern home for sale and the first people who went through it purchased it. The two properties closed within a week of each other.

It has now been 14 years since my husband's death and I am still living in my home. I truly believe that God and my husband joined together to help me through the hurting and helped me find this perfect home. I call it "Divine Intervention." My faith has grown stronger knowing someone up above is taking care of me.

The Spirit Whispered: Sorrow looks back. Worry looks around. Faith looks up.

Prayer: Divine Spirit, I find such comfort when I envision myself being taken by your hand and led on safe pathways. With your help, I am alert to potential problems and follow through with the appropriate action or inaction. You give me a gentle nudge in the right direction and surround me with your presence. There is no decision that I must make alone, for you are always with me. On the darkest night, you light my way. On the stormiest day, you provide me with shelter. Thank You, Holy Spirit!

Pauline Lynch
Retired Bank Vice President
Saginaw, MI

Whisper Twenty-One: A Son and Father Experience the Spirit

A Son's Tale

As I was sitting on a beach in the Outer Banks in North Carolina, I took out a book that one of my professors in college recommended. After reading the first few pages, I immediately called my father. I said, "Dad, stop everything you're doing and buy the book *Conversations with God* by Neale Donald Walsch." Without hesitation, he dropped what he was doing, went online, and purchased the book. I told him that the God in this book is the God that we have been searching for. I was humbly enlightened beyond belief by reading the first few pages. I was reading about God, but from a perspective that was unique and unknown; this was a God that taught that the Spirit was all around us, so much so that God and the Spirit are interchangeable.

I went back to my university a few days after this realization and continued reading and studying the Spirit. As a religion and philosophy major, I began to read my academic texts in a new light. I would share my newfound thoughts and experiences with my professors and they were open to listening; however, this God was not an academic God. I started to become enchanted because I understood this Spirit from a feeling center and was completely overwhelmed by its majesty.

I was inspired to experience life to its fullest glory. I was encouraged to never pray for supplication, but for gratitude. I was taught to love each and every living thing because the Spirit is in everything. And I realized that life was a process of creation.

All of these thoughts were rustling around in my mind, but what startled me the most was that for the first time I was feeling something of overwhelming power and I had no one to share it with. My professors were apathetic, friends disinterested, and there was only so much of this glory I could contain inside.

When my father and I were reunited during my winter break, we discussed these newly found ideas of how the Spirit was operating in our day-to-day lives. We both could not believe how much goes unnoticed; if only we had opened our eyes and hearts to the wonders of this world, we would have realized all that there is to be grateful for. The seemingly trivial things like awaking each morning, being at full health, having a roof above our heads and clothes on our bodies are extraordinary in and of themselves. Now take everything else that we had. I am not talking about materialistic possessions, but about the love of our family, the relationships with our friends, and the smiles of strangers. Abundance is everywhere.

Abundance was manifesting itself all the more between me and my father through us now knowing the Spirit. We had always had a special connection, but we now resonated with each other on a whole different plane. The familial love was always there, but now the spiritual love was present as well. It was as if we were always in sync. While together, there was always positivity, happiness and laughter. To top it all off, we were able to have religiously and spiritually stimulating conversations. We were not merely chattering, but engaging in philosophical discussions centered on how the Spirit was ever present. Having these conversations with my greatest role model, advocate, and supporter is a feeling that is indescribable. Although difficult to believe, my already flawless relationship with my father became divine.

When I was younger and unable to accurately articulate how I was feeling, I used to describe myself as a "Ping-Pong ball" bouncing back-and-forth between each parent. Being the product of divorce, I often felt as if there was this void that was never whole. I thought that since my family was not whole, I could never be whole. Both my parents were always supportive and I felt very loved. Nevertheless, the void remained.

The Spirit now fills that void with wonder and awe and to experience it with my father is all the more meaningful. Although it is hard to believe, since learning about the Spirit, I have realized that relationships are the greatest gift that we have. I can now truly know, experience, and be.

While reading **Conversations with God,** I was struck by one passage.

> "The grandest teaching of Christ was not that you shall have everlasting life—but that you do; not that you shall have brotherhood in God, but that you do; not that you shall have whatever you request, but that you do."

Unless we go within, we will most certainly go without. The Spirit has taught my father and me that we have unbounded potential and the ability to manifest the Spirit of God in our lives. We now live our lives with limitless joy and sheer love for all of the gifts that we are surrounded by. Just as Jesus says, we have all that it is we desire. We only need to peer beyond appearances to realize what it is we have.

The Spirit Whispered: Please continue to hear me with your heart. It responds better than when you just hear with your ears.

Prayer: Divine Spirit, I come to you with gratitude and humility. I am humbled by your everlasting presence and overjoyed to have come to realize you. With your abundance, I can do anything.

Andrew Luisi, a Business English Teacher in Germany,
who also blogs for *Huffington Post Religion*
on interfaith collaboration, multiculturalism and plurality.

A Father's Tale

As I was sitting at my computer at the studios of *Good Morning America*, my son called me and asked if I ever heard of the book, **Conversations with God** by Neale Donald Walsch. I said no. He told me to stop everything and buy the COMPLETE version, *an uncommon dialogue.* I did, as any good father would do. It changed my life. It made me start thinking. Who would have thought that a practicing Catholic for over 50 years, a church musician for 40 of those years, would be questioning his faith and become a seeker of God's holy truth...and his son would be his spiritual guide!

At 3:00, during my weekly visit with Jesus in the Perpetual Eucharistic Adoration chapel, I sat in the back row holding up the **Conversations with God** book and asked, "God, who are you? Are you the God in front of me in the monstrance, or are you the New God in this book? Or are you maybe both?"

I was taught that God was an all-powerful, judgmental, angry, jealous and vengeful God; if I didn't lead the life that he wanted me to lead on this earth, I would be punished for all eternity in the fires of hell! Whew, that's some tough God, but my God is a loving and accepting God. No matter what I do on this earth in my human body, my soul is destined to spend eternity with him in heaven. I questioned the whole concept of sin. Why would Jesus suffer and die on the cross for my sins if I'm still sinning? Even after I go to the Sacrament of Reconciliation, a week later...a day later...an hour later, I'm committing the same sins. It doesn't make any sense! When I took the word "sin" out of my life, I sinned less. I became a better person. I was just having human experiences.

We are not human beings having a spiritual experience.
We are spiritual beings having a human experience.
Teilhard de Chardin

So after reading all three volumes of **Conversations with God**, I craved more. I read more spiritual books, had more spiritual conversations with friends, then BAM! Andrew hit me with the documentary, "The Secret." If you haven't seen this, go on Netflix and see it! It's about the Law of Attraction...Positive Thinking...and Gratitude. Some of my friends told me to watch out, I was going in the wrong direction, but what's bad about positive thinking, gratitude and attracting the life that you want? Yes, "The Secret" uses the word universe in the film, but I just replace universe with God. My life has changed dramatically using **The Secret** and **Conversations with God,** and the many other spiritual books I have read, and my relationship with Andrew has taken on a new meaning. We are connected in a different way. We are connected in a spiritual way. We have deeper conversations and "Wow" moments when we come across a new message. I am more open to the Spirit. I have learned that the Spirit is inside of me... inside each of us.

Meditation books tell us to go deep within, where God dwells. It's the best advice in peaceful times and stressful times. I try to block out the world, go inside, and be grateful for what I have and what has been given to me over the years. It's like finding "heaven on earth!" We can create our own heaven or hell, by our actions. No need to explain that or give you examples, you've been there before. You know.

Live in the now. Don't beat yourself up with things in the past and don't worry about things in the future. Live for "heaven on earth" now! Decide to love, be patient, be kind. Simplify your life. Spend more time with your family and friends. Read more, take a walk, and listen to music. You've read this before in other books. I'm not telling you anything new.

Eat right, sleep more, exercise, drink plenty of water, meditate, slow down, relax...you know what to do. I've worked at *Good Morning America* for over 29 years and met many self-help professionals who gave their advice on how to make you a better person. God bless them, but find what's right for you, what makes you happy, and do it!

I love the stars and the moon. I feel a connection with them. Each morning when I leave my house for work, I gaze up into the universe and say good morning to God. "I offer this day for you."

On a clear night, I usually see three stars in a row, one star shining brighter than the other. In my Catholic upbringing, I would see the Holy Trinity: Father, Son and Holy Spirit, but in my new spirituality I see: Father (Me), Son (Andrew) and the Holy Spirit (God), and I feel the connection with Andrew who is almost 6,000 miles away while he is studying in Jerusalem. I have been a church musician for over 40 years, leading the music at Mass, retreats, conferences and concerts, but Andrew is walking in the steps of Jesus. How cool is that, and he's sharing his life with me and his new found spirituality.

In addition to the stars, when I see the moon, I feel a special connection with God. It's a reassuring moment when God says everything is okay. You are on the right path. And when I see a beautiful full moon, it reminds me of the Holy Eucharist. I can never leave my Catholic roots. They are a part of me, but the Spirit has guided me in a new direction. I have "Opened the Eyes of My Heart" and I see God in everything. I am blessed and so are YOU.

The Spirit Whispered: You are Special. I love you. Look within no matter what religion or spirituality you may be. I am there. Be open to all, accepting and loving.

Prayer: Divine Spirit, thank you for being my guide. Thank you for being my friend. Thank you for being my all. Bless me and my family so we may be a blessing to others.

Eddie Luisi, Stage Manager for *Good Morning America*
church musician, songwriter, producer, composer and publisher
with his company: Faith, Family and Friends Music
New York, NY

Whisper Twenty-Two: Father's Voice

There is usually nothing more comforting than the sound of your father's voice. For so many years that was true for me. I was the first child to live after six failed deliveries. You can imagine how I was welcomed into my family. Like so many other little girls, I just loved my dad. I followed him everywhere, chatting away constantly. Life took a sad turn however, as my parents began to argue more and more. My father was often angry and seemed to disconnect from the family. Sometimes he didn't return home at night. A few days would pass before he'd return with no explanation. He certainly didn't seem happy to be with us.

Before long it became easier for his children, now consisting of three girls and a boy, to be in bed when he would finally come home. We didn't understand. The days of singing "together" became fewer and fewer and then finally disappeared. As a teenager, I understood how to love someone and not like him. The pain was raw and deep. I guess, he didn't love us anymore. The sound of my father's voice became one to cause fear and not support. I knew I still loved him. I would stay awake for hours so I could be sure that he made it home safely.

After college, I returned home and found the quiet deafening. Even the yelling had stopped. Every now and then his voice could make us laugh as he shared a story, joke or sang a song. He was charismatic when he wanted to be. He still had the power to fix situations. If you could talk to him, he seemed to have the power to fix or help. Eventually, my parents separated and a couple days later my father died. I cried deeply that day. I cried not just for the present loss but the loss of the potential he wasted, the blessings he took for granted.

Many years later, I was in a serious car accident, hitting a pole head-on. It happened so quickly that I don't remember the impact, but when I opened my eyes my hands were full of blood. I couldn't focus and honestly didn't know what had happened. Anxiety filled my heart as I tried to gain consciousness. Then I heard my father's voice, "You are all right. I am here. Don't be afraid." I felt safe.

Amazingly, I only broke my nose but totaled the car. I thanked God for watching over me, but sometimes I have felt that he was too busy to listen to me.

A few years later I had another accident, more serious this time. While fixing a favorite recipe, a pot of boiling cooking oil fell down my leg and onto my foot. An ambulance was called. I was dizzy with pain and began to feel as if I might slip away or faint. I heard a voice call out, "I am here. Do not be afraid, you will be all right."

Morphine was administered causing the pain to cease, but I could remember feeling a hand on my shoulder. "It will be all right." It was my father's voice. I had heard that same voice before, loud and clear. Then I remembered my car accident. It was that same voice: reassuring, strong, filling my heart with a sense of peace. This time though I realized that the voice I heard was not my biological father's voice. It was my heavenly Father.

These three events have taught me to listen more intently. My heavenly Father has spoken to me often throughout my life and continues to do so. I now know I need to listen.

The Spirit Whispered: I am always here for you. Never be afraid. Just trust in me and listen to me.

Prayer: Divine Spirit, I am grateful. You know all that goes on in my life. You have been there, whispering "I am here" in those desperate times, but also in the joyful times as well. Thank you for your care and the steady sound of your voice calling me, helping me to learn how to listen.

Angela Robben
Bible Study Leader
Ann Arbor, MI

Whisper Twenty-Three: Lost and Found

In December 2008, my future husband got down on one knee in front of his entire family and proposed to me. I was ecstatic, emotional, and overwhelmed with joy. Failing to recognize he was trying to place a beautiful diamond ring on my finger, I excitedly hugged him and flailed my arms about. The ring was absolutely gorgeous, the most prized possession I had ever owned. I could see the concern in my new fiancé's eyes as he said, "Monica, please just don't lose this ring!"

I had a reputation for misplacing items: my phone, my keys, my purse, jewelry, and money—you name it; I had lost it. I looked at my future husband and said, "I promise, this is one thing I WILL NOT lose!"

In 2010, we became husband and wife and have since welcomed two precious daughters into our family. Over the years, my reputation for keeping track of my personal belongings has improved only *slightly.*

In December 2013, five years after the proposal, I noticed on my way to work that I had forgotten to put on my engagement ring and wedding band. Since I remove the rings each evening and place them on the bathroom counter, I didn't think much of it. The next day, I noticed again that my rings were missing from my finger. When I got home, I checked the bathroom and could not find the rings anywhere. I looked on my night stand, other bathrooms, the kitchen, my drawers, my purse and even the car. I wondered what else I could have done with the rings!

I said a prayer to St. Anthony, patron saint of lost items, and decided they must be somewhere in the house. I figured they would turn up eventually. A few days went by with more sporadic looking. I even asked my three-year-old daughter, "Did you do anything with Mommy's special rings?" Her story changed several times and I decided her information was unreliable!

Once again I asked for guidance from God, prayed for the intercession of St. Anthony, and trusted that I would find them without having to search through every nook and cranny of the house! This went on for about three weeks. I reassured my husband that the rings would be found, although my track record gave him cause for skepticism. I admit that I was also having flashes of doubt.

On New Year's Eve, my husband and I booked a babysitter for the girls and attended a party in town. Before we left, I sadly looked at my bare left ring finger, praying again for direction in finding the meaningful treasures that I had lost. After arriving at the party, it dawned on me that I had left something important at home! I felt frustrated once again by my forgetfulness, and irritated that because of this ever-present imperfection, I had to leave the party for a time.

Alone in the house, I walked through my bedroom and into the bathroom. As I did this, I heard a very clear and unmistakable voice say to me, "Go through the trash. Your rings are in there." I eyed the overstuffed trash can, which is normally emptied by my husband on a regular basis. Again I heard the clear statement repeated, "Your rings are in there." With a mixture of excitement and doubt, I hesitantly began pulling items out of the trash. About halfway through the process, I froze as I caught sight of my rings. They were glimmering, shining and still bringing the truth of God's love to my heart. I fell to my knees and thanked God, as tears streamed down my face.

When I shared the wonderful news with my husband, he was overcome with relief. He also revealed that he had *almost* emptied the bathroom trash several times over the past couple weeks. He opted not to on multiple occasions as the outdoor garbage bins were too full, or he didn't have time. I believe he was prevented by something much greater.

The Spirit Whispered: Your concerns matter to me. I am always with you. I use your weaknesses to draw you nearer to me. Listen to me.

Prayer: Divine Spirit, increase my awareness of your movement around me and your strength within me. May my imperfections bring me closer to you this day.

Monica Poff
Social Worker
Lansing, MI

―――――――――・・―――――――――

"Dear God, I need you to fill me with excitement once again. Please awaken my Spirit. I feel like I have been out of focus and asleep for so long, Lord wake me up and return me to the land of the living."

Karen Kostyla

―――――――――・・―――――――――

Whisper Twenty-Four: The Ten Dollar Bill

The bar on Westnedge Road was dimly lit as I sat alone drinking a pint of beer in the early afternoon. I was the only person sitting at the bar. Recently, I had begun to feel that my life was spiraling out of control as the drinking had slowly progressed over the past months and my money dwindled.

But today was different. This was a new type of low. As I drank the beer, I looked into the mirror adorning the backdrop of the bar. I looked old for my age; bloated with an unkempt beard and scraggly hair. It had been months since I really looked at myself in the mirror. I found the sight of my face unbearable, but even worse were the memories of my disgraceful actions.

I was drunk, but lucid enough to realize all that I had done wrong. I pulled seventeen dollars out of my pocket and looked at the front of the ten dollar bill. It was only a ten dollar bill, but it's how it came into my possession that fueled a feeling of guilt. It was what the bill represented that troubled me.

The previous day I had stolen that ten dollar bill from a friend's nightstand; a friend who trusted me enough to go into her home and care for her animals. She hadn't realized yet that I had stolen it. As I stared closely at the bill that I was going to use to feed my addiction, an overwhelming sense of anger and shame came over me. I had become a thief. I considered myself evil. I had allowed alcohol to make the decisions in my life; I was going to cast aside the trust built between two individuals to pay for another drink.

I began to tear up as I looked at the front of the crumpled ten dollar bill. What had I done? What kind of path was I choosing in life? To make matters worse, without the money, I wouldn't be able to pay my bill. I had a decision to make: pay the bill with the stolen money or ask if there was another way I could pay.

I didn't know what to do. I turned over the ten dollar bill and looked at the back. I hadn't paid much attention before, but looking closely at it, the words, "In God We Trust," glared at me. I had lost faith following high school, but I stared at those words and silently asked God for guidance. And he provided.

The bartender, seeing the tears in my eyes, asked, "Is everything okay?"

"Just having a rough day," I replied.

I had made the decision to tell my friend what I had done and return the money to her, choosing at that moment to face the consequences of not having enough money to pay the bartender.

"Would you like another drink?" he asked.

"No, thank you," I said. I garnered up the courage and asked, "Is there any way I can pay you later or can I work it off or something? I don't have enough money right now to pay the bill."

"Listen, I know you come in here a lot and that you're a good customer. Today's bill is on me," he said.

I was shocked at this sentiment, at his kindness toward me. But it made me feel worse, as I was undeserving of such a gesture, of such pity. I insisted that I somehow pay, but he insisted otherwise.

"God says we should take care of one another, especially in our times of need," he said as I repeatedly thanked him. I left the bar with those words replaying in my mind.

The following day when my friend returned from vacation, I told her what I had done and returned the money. I wholeheartedly apologized and instead of being angry or disappointed, she was appreciative of my honesty. She told me that righting wrongs showed character and it took courage to face the consequences of my actions.

When I received my next paycheck, I went to the bar to pay my bill. Again, the bartender insisted I keep it, but knowing the truth of my actions, I couldn't possibly accept his kindness. I told him my story, and what his words and actions meant to me. I handed him fifty dollars.

He handed the money back, smiled, and said, "Take the money and do something good for someone else."

The Spirit Whispered: Trust in me to see the light even in the darkest of days. I am always right there beside you, whether in words or actions, if you choose to see me.

Prayer: Divine Spirit, although I may sometimes neglect you as I walk the path of my life, I wish to thank you for not abandoning me in my toughest times and for always guiding me back to you.

Kenneth Francis Pearson, Graduate Student
Fairleigh Dickinson University
Blooming Grove, NY

---

*"Today I will ask myself
what I really want
and listen to
the whispers of my soul."*

The Gossamer Path

Whisper Twenty-Five: The Missed Kiss

It was just after midnight on a Saturday night in January when we got the call no parent ever wants to receive. Ryan, our oldest son, had been hit by a car while walking across campus with some of his buddies and had been taken by ambulance to the hospital. My husband, Randy, answered the phone as he was still up playing computer games. I had gone to bed about an hour earlier. Randy woke me, and the sense of dread on his face registered before his words and I hopped out of bed. We rushed to dress and then headed for the hospital. We were grateful for the dry roads that allowed us to travel at full speed.

Earlier that evening, I was at my desk plugging away on some work emails. Our younger son, Drew, had already left the house to spend the night with a friend. Ryan, who had turned 21 earlier that month, was going over to his girlfriend's aunt's house for dinner. I had plans to visit my friend, Janice, for the evening to enjoy some pizza, wine and a movie. Because we sometimes cracked open a second bottle of wine when we got together, I had asked Randy to drive me to Janice's house which was about five miles away.

I pushed back from my desk about 6 p.m. and got ready to leave. I called downstairs to Ryan to say goodbye, and when he didn't res-pond, Randy said he must have already left for dinner. Immediately, I was unsettled. Ever since my boys had begun driving, I had a tradition of kissing them on the cheek as they were leaving the house and saying, "Be safe."

"He can't be gone," I said to Randy. "He didn't say goodbye and he never leaves without saying goodbye." Randy assured me that Ryan had probably been in a hurry when Katie picked him up and just said "Bye" as he was running out the door, which we failed to hear.

"Please go downstairs and check his room," I said, still stymied. And he did, acknowledging as he came up the stairs that no one was home but us. On the way to Janice's, I badgered Randy again—"Did you look on both sides of his bed while you were downstairs?" I asked, thinking that Ryan might have mysteriously passed out and was lying where he could not have been seen from the bedroom door.

"Yes, Margaret, I looked all over the room," Randy said. "Quit worrying about it."

I enjoyed a four-hour visit with Janice, drinking just one bottle of wine, watching a two-hour comedy special and laughing out loud. I was tired and went straight to bed when I got home. I woke up suddenly about an hour later with Randy standing at the foot of the bed.

"Margaret, get up," he said. "Ryan's been in a car accident. He's at Bronson Hospital. Jeremy just called."

That was enough to get me moving at warp speed, but I was too petrified to ask Randy what had happened. Once we were in the car and on our way, I sheepishly asked Randy if Ryan had been in his own car or in one of his friend's cars when the accident occurred.

"No, he was walking across Howard Street and got hit by a car," Randy said.

I began screaming, "Oh, my God, oh, my God." I envisioned the worst scenarios.

Now, I needed some measure of the extent of Ryan's injuries and mustered the courage to ask, "Was he able to talk after he was hit?" I asked, every muscle in my body tightly torqued.

"Yes, Jeremy said Ryan responded when the paramedics asked him questions," Randy said.

We drove the rest of the 11 miles to the hospital in silence. I was afraid to think or talk about what we might have to face this night, or whether our son would be with us when tomorrow arrived. As a lifelong practicing Christian, I always turned to prayer in times of trouble. I began a silent litany of Our Fathers with the wish that all of us be filled with the power of the Holy Spirit. I concentrated on my breaths and prayer while Randy concentrated on driving.

When we arrived at the hospital, four of Ryan's friends were sitting in the emergency waiting room, along with the parents of one of the boys. These young men were all unabashedly crying, I had to tap into strength. I had just prayed to be strong and comfort them as they told us what had happened.

After having dinner with his girlfriend's family, Ryan met up with his buddies to go to a party. About midnight, they decided to walk to a restaurant, which would require crossing a multi-lane road. Ryan, at the head of the pack, crossed the southbound lanes of traffic and two lanes of cars at red lights waiting to turn left. He mistakenly stepped out into the through lane which had a green light. Suddenly, the boys right behind him saw Ryan get clipped by a car bumper (going 35 mph), flip onto the car hood, slam his head in the windshield, and then he was thrown from the car into the middle of the intersection. An infusion of grace helped me to listen without weeping as we waited with them.

Finally, Randy and I were able to see Ryan. We experienced a mixture of joy and despair when we first saw him with the neurosurgeon who would, in just a couple hours, attempt to fix the leaking brain fluid caused by Ryan's cracked skull. His head and right leg (he had broken both calf bones) were covered with huge bandages. He looked at us and he knew we were his parents. Our hearts filled with hope when Ryan was able to tell the doctor the name of the current U.S. President, his birthday, and where he was.

We kissed him and sent him off for pre-surgery prep. We headed home about four a.m. for a quick shower and fresh clothes as we knew that we had a long and challenging day ahead.

It was too early to call anyone, so I never stopped praying all the way home, alternating between talking to my God and calling on the Blessed Mother to watch over Ryan. When we arrived home, I showered, which helped me refocus from the surreal experience of being in the ER in the middle of the night.

Everything was out of our control, but the Holy Spirit shored me up and kept me from collapsing into the gut-wrenching sobs that hovered over me for the next week or so. I sensed I needed to let go. I had never before been able to turn something over to God so confidently.

"God," I said out loud. "If it's Ryan's time to go, please make it as pain-free and peaceful as possible. If it's not his time to go, know I will love and cherish him every day for the rest of his life, just as I always have."

With that, I felt my body relax into the seat, the what-if frenzy in my head calmed, and the agitation in my stomach dissipated. Never in my life had I experienced such tangible, immediate comfort from prayer. It became apparent to me that whatever happened to Ryan, I would be able to handle it with this bountiful grace I had tapped into via prayer.

Several hours later, Ryan was out of surgery. The neurosurgeon pointed to the heavens and said, "Someone up there likes this guy a lot," acknowledging that Ryan was extremely lucky to have survived such intense injuries to his head. He stayed in the trauma unit for 11 days with a steady stream of visiting family, friends and local Catholic clergy.

I remained strong for Ryan all day, then wept on the 11-mile trip back home every night, even when it was very clear that Ryan would likely make a full recovery. After a second surgery—this time on his broken leg—we took Ryan home. His leg took 15 months and a skin graft to recover. Ryan suffered no long term damage other than the horseshoe scar on his skull and the ones on his leg.

I had been a practicing Catholic for 46 years when Ryan was hit by that car and until then, I never had my faith so tested. I still marvel that I was able to utter that simple prayer placing Ryan in God's hand. That experience was an epiphany about the deep vault of comfort and guidance my faith could lend to my life.

The Spirit Whispered: Breathe, he's cradled in my arms.

Prayer: Divine Spirit, Thank you for being the "magnet" in my life who is always invisibly guiding me to give and seek your truth, justice, comfort and love. I promise to be attentive to your tug and continue to move ever closer to you.

Margaret von Steinen, Poet, Writer, International Communications
Officer, Western Michigan University
Kalamazoo, MI

———————— ◆ ————————

"For it was not into my ear you whispered,
but into my heart.
It was not my lips you kissed,
but my soul."

Judy Garland

———————— ◆ ————————

Whisper Twenty-Six: The Spirit Whispered...This Is Not The One!

One day after John and I were engaged, we went looking for our first apartment that we would share as a newly married couple. We had very little knowledge of the vast city of Minneapolis, other than this was where we would go to graduate school (the University of Minnesota) and begin our married life.

We had come to Minnesota to visit our extended family and had only one day to find our apartment. My future father-in-law insisted on joining us for this adventure. We began first thing in the morning with a long drive and an appointment at an apartment search agency that helped us narrow our choices. (Please note this was before Google and online searches.)

With our list, a map, and much hope, we set off. We quickly found that it would be a challenge to find an apartment we were comfortable with and could afford within walking a distance to the University of Minnesota. After an exhausting day, we finally found one and signed the rental agreement. It was very exciting for us to formally sign the rental agreement that we would enter into as husband and wife! We drove back to St. Cloud, MN, which was about an hour north of Minneapolis, with growing excitement and anticipation at the thought of returning to our first home as husband and wife!

Unbeknownst to us, as we were driving north, management had made the decision not to honor the terms of our rental agreement. We received this news upon our return. We were very disappointed but even more astonished that they were able to find us (this was before cell phones). The only contact information the manager had was our information from Michigan. It seems that the agent we were dealing with remembered that we had talked about St. Cloud. So they began calling people with the surname Bursch until they found my fiance's grandmother. We were devastated by the news and nearly out of time!

We canceled our plans for the next day and borrowed my future father-in-law's car to return to Minneapolis. We prayed as we drove and wondered what we would do if we couldn't find a place. We returned to a few complexes we had seen the day before and felt uncertain about what to do. Nothing felt just right, but we were also feeling desperate to secure an apartment. We stopped to discuss our options. We were really choosing between two apartments about two blocks apart. They seemed pretty indistinguishable except for the fact that one was a much larger complex. We decided to go with the large complex, Complex A. We went to a corner store and pulled out a quarter to use the pay phone. As we stood there at the side of the store with the quarter hovering at the slot, John uttered a quick prayer that God would lead us to the right apartment. He dropped the quarter in and dialed the apartment complex manager. As John began to explain our situation and asked to come over to sign an agreement, the phone went dead.

We looked at each other in disbelief! How could this be? We both just knew we needed to go to the smaller complex. In utter astonishment, we hurriedly walked to the complex and were thankful to find the manager in. He welcomed us into his office/apartment. As we stood there discussing the availability and terms, John and I both noticed a print of the "Footprints in the Sand" poem, which was near an "Our Father" print. We squeezed each other's hand, reassuring each other silently that this was where God wanted us to be. We signed the rental agreement and headed back to St. Cloud with renewed joy and expectation as we thought about beginning our married life in Minneapolis!

Postscript: We moved into our first apartment on University Avenue in August 1994. In a very short time we knew, without a doubt, that God had led us to the right place. Numerous times in the first few weeks alone, the police were called to Complex A for partying, drugs, and fighting. Not once did that happen at our small, quiet complex during the two years we lived there. Thank you, Jesus!

The Spirit Whispered: This is not the right apartment for you. Trust me! I know a better place for the two of you to begin married life.

Prayer: Divine Spirit, thank you for your guidance in the choices we face in our lives. Thank you for keeping our hearts open to the signs you provide, subtle or not so subtle—like a phone going dead in mid-conversation!

Angela Bursch
Wife and Mother [5 children]
Caledonia, MI

"Trust me."
The words came as a
gentle whisper
to her soul.

Author Unknown

Whisper Twenty-Seven: A Heart's Adventure

It seems that as a young woman, I was looking for a relationship that made me feel better, one that made me feel whole; a relationship that made me feel more like the person that God had called me to be. I came to the realization that I was not in that type of relationship. My friend was a fine man, with character and strong interests, but we did not make each other better. We were living parallel lives instead of building a life together. After coming to this realization, it was actually quite easy for both of us to let the relationship fade.

The problem was, I was no longer a couple; instead I was a single woman trying to take my life back. I had become sedentary and dependent on someone else for my happiness. I started visiting friends again, began working out and eating well to make my body feel whole. I invited the Spirit into my life for guidance and direction. I made sure my heart was open to others as well as a willingness to allow others to help me to become better. And, it didn't take long.

I decided it was time to get back to dating and wanted to see what kind of men were out there. Being a child of the digital age, instead of going to the bar, I went to my trusty Internet to see what I could find. Joining online dating was scary but also very interesting. I was able to write down exactly who I was, what I was looking for, and what my expectations of a relationship were. Then I could sit back and wait to see if anyone would match my search. I joined this online dating site on a Saturday, and a few people were interested in my profile but no one seemed to fit the lifestyle I was looking for.

The next day, I received a message from someone whose profile intrigued me. There were pictures of him rock climbing, biking, skiing, and one picture of him showed an amazing smile. We started talking and right away I felt like something was different. He was honest, sincere in his questions; plus he was interested in doing things instead of just sitting around watching hockey. We booked our first date for that Wednesday. We were going to play miniature golf, meeting in a public place, just in case things didn't work out.

By the end of the night, we had really bonded. Neither of us wanted to leave.

Even though I was searching for someone special, I could not have imagined the type of man God was going to bring to me. The Spirit guided me to a place of strength and helped me realize that I did not need someone to help me be me. I wanted someone to help me be better. After a year and four months of serious adventure, I was sure this was the man for me. We spent that time: rock climbing in the mountains, biking, camping, making new friends together, driving 15,000 km [9,300 miles] from Alberta to Newfoundland and learning how to support, and encourage each other to be the best person we could be. This man was no longer just someone I met online; instead he was the one that the Spirit led me to find.

Thanksgiving weekend, we escaped to the mountains to go climbing. After about 30 minutes of hiking we arrived at the base of the climb. I started to unpack all of my gear and Chris came to sit next to me. After saying how much he loved me, he asked me to marry him. My response was, "Yes!"

To be honest, I knew that the question was coming, but it still felt amazing to have the chance to say yes to someone who I knew would help me be a better person. He was definitely the one I wanted to spend the rest of my life with exploring together, supporting each other, and LITERALLY climbing mountains together!

The Spirit Whispered: Trust me. There is a route I will take you to find the way to tackle any mountain you wish to climb.

Prayer: Divine Spirit, help me to rely on your plan and to focus on today. Thank you for the clarity and understanding that has brought me to this place where I can love, be loved, and rely on love. I am looking forward to the places you will guide us to. Help us to be present to the many views of God's creation along the way.

Breanne Lowe, Teacher
Edmonton, Alberta, Canada

Whisper Twenty-Eight: Live and Love Fully with Your Whole Heart

Although I was raised in a strong Catholic family, wore plaid skirts and knee socks for my first eight years of schooling, and rarely missed a Sunday Mass, I can't exactly say that my personal faith has always been rock solid. Sure, I knew the order of the Mass like the back of my hand and could recite nearly any prayer in my sleep without skipping a beat, but those were just the motions. As far as actually *believing* in what I was doing and saying? That was another story.

There has never been a point in time when I didn't believe in God— or in some higher power for that matter. I've never completely *lost* my faith. But I never really had a faith to begin with. When I say faith I'm referring to a belief in something much greater than anything on this earth, a deep connection or *relationship* with some higher being. Something you can feel in the depths of your heart ...something unexplainable, something real.

I was never quite sure about the whole "divine plan" thing, I didn't completely buy into the idea of angels and I had a very hard time with the notion of trusting someone or something that I couldn't even see. I tend to be a tad perfectionist, I like to be in control, and I'd rather not depend on anyone. So any thought of "letting go" and placing complete trust in some far off higher power didn't sit well with me. I *wanted* the kind of strong faith that I had learned about in school: the kind of reassuring faith that wiped anxiety and worry away, the kind that left no room for fear and the kind that allowed life to be a beautiful adventure. But I couldn't seem to grasp it. It just seemed too good to be true. Until three days ago.

On the Fourth of July, I lost a very special person in a tragic ATV accident. Her name was Katie Paul and, to me, she was so much more than a dear friend. She was family.

Growing up, Katie and I spent our summers together. We lived two doors down from each other in northern Michigan on a private lake. What began as friendly neighbors soon blossomed into a remarkable friendship not only between us but also between our two close-knit and crazily similar families. Over time, her uncle became mine and mine became hers. We each gained an extra set of grandparents, and the last names Bade and Paul became synonymous.

Katie was the perfect exemplification of her family. She was hard working, dependable, down to earth, full of faith, and overflowing with life. Family and faith were her top priorities, and she would drop *everything* in order to be there for the ones she loved. She never took herself too seriously and her sense of humor was unparalleled. She treated each day like the gift that it was. She was fearless, and when she wanted something she went after it. She knew that real happiness is not a destination but a journey to be enjoyed. And she knew that the true value in life does not come from tangible things but from the people you meet and the lives you touch along the way.

As painful as it is to come to grips with such a loss, I can't help but recognize the divine impact that my friend had on this world. She had that sparkle, that zest for life, that "impossible" faith that I was convinced was too good to be true.

The night of her death, my family and I were sitting around our campfire late at night still in shock from the news. The fireworks had ceased and activity on the lake was slim to none. Suddenly, a cabin light directly across the lake came on to reveal a perfect silhouette of a freestanding cross in the yard and the beams of light were clearly visible, piercing through the darkness behind the cross...but there was nothing in that yard to cause such a shadow. It lasted only a minute or so before going completely dark. My dad, brother, step-mom and I all saw it at the same time and it absolutely took our breath away. With that, you can bet that my insecurity and doubts about my faith were no more.

Through Katie, the Spirit showed me that strong faith does exist and that although life is fragile, it is beautiful. Katie's life and death reminded me to live with purpose and intention and to invest in people rather than things.

The Spirit Whispered: Give thanks each day. Live and love fully with your whole heart.

Prayer: Divine Spirit, remind me each and every day to be thankful for all of my blessings and to live my life to the fullest. Help me to harness the same beautiful energy that Katie Paul showed the world. Allow me to keep her funny, fearless, loving spirit alive as it is truly a reflection of you.

Meghan Elizabeth Bade, Kinesiology Major
Michigan State University
East Lansing, MI

―――― • ――――

*"Each whisper from your heart
is a potential boarding pass
for the next leg of your journey
that is your life.
Where will you fly to next?"*

Author Unknown

―――― • ――――

Whisper Twenty-Nine: I Will Never Forget You

"I will never forget you my people. I have carved you in the palm of my hand." Isaiah 49: 15-16

I was raised a Catholic, went to a Catholic school for twelve years, and was a rule-follower. I went on to become an elementary school teacher which was a dream that I held close to my heart since childhood.

After my junior year in college, I met who I thought was the love of my life. We were married a year after I graduated. We didn't have much when we started out, but we had each other and I had my faith.

After five years of marriage, I gave birth to my first son, Jamie. Three years later I gave birth to my second son, Ryan. When Jamie was four years old, he died. It was sudden and there was no time to prepare (if you ever can) for such a tragedy. During the week when he was in a coma, I asked the Lord to restore my little boy and make him well again. I remembered a lesson from grade school that I had never forgotten about prayers being answered. The sister said, "If you live a good life and you pray for something that's not important, God might not answer your prayer. But if you pray for something that is important, God will answer your prayer." I prayed so hard that Jamie would come back to me, but he died the day before my thirty-first birthday.

At first, I didn't blame God. I was too numb to even think. One day at the Christian book store while sifting through books on loss and grief, I looked up and found a plaque with the words from the book of Isaiah. It was three dimensional with a child being held in the palm of God's hand. Underneath the sculpture, it read, **I will never forget you...I have carved you in the palm of my hand.** It held two messages for me. First and foremost, the child repre-sented Jamie, my little angel, who I would never forget. The hand was the Hand of God, caring for my child until the day I would be called back home. Secondly, I wanted to believe that God wouldn't forget about me, and would hold me in the palm of his hand during this unbearable time of sadness. But the grief was overtaking me, and I started to spiral downward. I began questioning why God had taken my child and didn't answer my prayer. I began to blame him. I was very angry with him. *"I will never forget you, my people."* Really?

Some of the children that I taught had parents who were alcoholics, drug dealers, and prostitutes. God didn't take their children. What about the children who came home to an empty apartment after school, only to find their meager possessions strewn on the street. Their mother was nowhere to be found. She left after being evicted, leaving the children to fend for themselves.

Or what about the child who came to school with bruises, crying because his mother's boyfriend had beaten him. The list goes on. Wouldn't it have been better for God to take those children and give them the peace and the love that they deserved? Why mine? I was a good parent and felt that I was doing what God had asked me to do.

After years of grief counseling, my marriage failed. You know those dreams about growing old together, and having a house full of grandchildren to love? Well, that dream would never become a reality.

I had lost my son. I had lost my husband. I had lost my faith. I stopped going to church. **"I will never forget you my people."** **Those words were meant for someone else, NOT ME!**

My parents, who attended Mass on a regular basis, encouraged me to go back to church. Eventually, I went to a non-denominational church for a while, but soon lost interest. I was still feeling overwhelmed. Not only did I have a full-time job that never seemed to end, but I was also responsible for all the work at home that is usually shared by two people. Besides, I needed my rest on Sunday mornings. This went on for years.

My younger son, Ryan, eventually moved to Chicago for an education and a job in the fashion industry. He has lived there for ten years. Even though we talk to each other at least three times a week and visit each other when we can, it is not the same as having your child live near you.

Once Ryan had moved away, I buried myself in my work. I was now working in an affluent school district after being laid off and recalled several times from the previous school district.

I went back to the Catholic Church once again when my aging father came to stay with me on weekends. I went to church for him, not for me. My attendance lasted for a little over two years.

Even during my years of disenchantment with this God who I believed abandoned me, I still believed in his existence and would ask for small favors once in a while. I guess I was testing him. I actually talked to my son Jamie more often than God, asking him to keep his brother in Chicago safe from harm. I always reassured Jamie that I still loved him, missed him and would never forget him.

One day, one of my students invited me to her church to see her in a skit. The skit took place before the service. Not wanting to disappoint her, I went. I was moved by what I saw and what I heard, but I didn't commit to the church.

During the course of the school year, I had several encounters with her parents. They were never reluctant to speak about their faith in God and always seemed so happy having a relationship with God. I wished that I had the faith they had.

At the end of that school year, I retired. There was a voice inside me that could not be quieted. "*Find a church. You need to know who I am.*" I went back to the church my student attended. The theme of the lesson was, "Who is God?" After the first service, I was hooked. I felt like the pastor was speaking directly to me. For the past two years, I have attended services regularly.

I was invited to become part of a small bible study group. I knew that this was another urging by the Spirit, so I willingly accepted the invitation. My faith has deepened and continues to do so through my affiliation with these people of faith. Collectively, this group has been the life preserver that has kept me afloat as we study, pray, serve those in need and enjoy a profound sense of community. Through my church and my new friends, I have learned that God has not forgotten me and he continues to hold me in the palm of his hand.

The Spirit Whispered: I have not forgotten you. Listen to the words you hear, and do as I ask. I have been with you through it all and have never abandoned you. I am waiting for you to return to me.

Prayer: Divine Spirit, you have urged me throughout my life to seek the truth and let go of the anger I harbored. I now realize how often you spoke the same message that had fallen on deaf ears. Thank you for the angels you have placed in my life to lighten my burden and lead me back to you.

Kathleen O'Neill
Retired Elementary School Teacher
Clinton Township, MI

Whisper Thirty: My 'Baptism' in the Jordan

All I heard was, "You've got six years to live. It's a special kind of mutation of a chromosome in your bone marrow. Your healthy bone marrow cells are being replaced by these mutated cells. The average lifespan once you have been diagnosed with this illness is about six years; give or take."

"That couldn't be right," I said to myself as I left my doctor's office. "He said, average, so it could be nine years. Besides, they may have a cure by then."

I spent the next two years going to homeopaths, herbalists, chiro-practors, and other health professionals who were trained in different forms of medical treatment. I was hopeful, though not op-timistic, that the treatments I'd receive from these alternative medical practitioners would stop the advance of this cancer that was running rampant throughout my bone marrow.

I was getting sicker. Fortunately, my naturopath was a good listener. As my anxiety increased, she would suggest various extracts that would help suppress my anxiety. In spite of those remedies, my anxiety continued to increase. As she was offering yet another possible extract, I interrupted her. "It won't help," I blurt-ed. "The anxiety is about my fear... and *that's* the problem. I have to deal with my fear of death; not just with my efforts to stop this disease."

She wisely responded, "When the student is ready, the teacher will appear."

I began attending church again. I had fallen away some time ago. I loved mass so much that I went daily, even though I attended a public school. Eventually I became an altar boy. For two years, during fifth and sixth grades, I never missed a day of Mass. My life, at that time, was very happy. I felt that Jesus was always with me, a good friend, no matter what I was doing.

The easy answer to my 'falling away' was puberty. I wouldn't have realized it then. It was just that I was really interested in girls and everything that an innocent youth wanted to explore. What terrified me the most about this interest was that it seemed to conflict with what I was taught about God. "Evil thoughts are as harmful as evil deeds," I was told. "If you die with that sin on your soul, you will go directly to hell."

Frankly, by the time I was in college, it seemed impossible to avoid hell—given the standard I believed was operating in the universe. It was easier (though I wasn't aware of this at the time) to stop going to church than to face the terror of hell.

Now, however, I was facing the terror of hell. In my adult life I had married, divorced and remarried. My soul was so tarnished with broken promises and broken hearts, that I assumed heaven was out of the question for me.

Once again I began attending church. Every week I'd argue with myself: "You hypocrite! You don't believe half the things the Catholic Church teaches. You're just going because you are scared and want to get on God's 'good side' before you die."

One Sunday, a voice within me settled that argument with this truth: "I don't go to church to worship the Catholic faith; I go to church to find my friendship with Jesus." Argument settled.

One week, Fr. Bernie from Manresa Jesuit Retreat Center in Detroit, touched me deeply with his sermon about the love of God the Father. Jesus called God the Father "Abba," a term of intimate and personal love for one's "Papa." This term was part of the culture in which Jesus lived. "He is a loving Daddy, who holds us on his chest and loves us as sons and daughters."

I told Fr. Bernie how much his message meant to me and that I wanted to learn more about the God he knew. He suggested that we see each other every other week. In the meantime, he gave me readings from the Bible to contemplate. He taught me about Imaginative Prayer. When one enters into Imaginative Prayer, one doesn't just 'read' the Bible; one enters the story one is reading about. You go back in time and enter the scene being described; asking yourself, "What do I see, hear, taste, smell and touch" in this world into which I'm allowing my mind to travel?

Father Bernie and I spent months together as I read and noted my thoughts and feelings about the Scripture verses he assigned for my contemplation. I was seeing God the Father in a new light as I experienced these readings. Consequently, Father Bernie offered me the opportunity to experience "The Spiritual Exercises of St. Ignatius" in the fall of 2006. This is a special 30-week long (give or take) replication of the spiritual process St. Ignatius (founder of the Jesuits) experienced in his conversion—and one he developed throughout his life to help others 'experience' the realities of God the Father, God the Son, and God the Holy Spirit.

The first eight weeks of these exercises were life changing for me. Somehow, inexplicably, I received the grace I prayed for each week. There were times when I was tearful, joyful, frightened, but always moved deeply by my experience with the Scriptural text and my imagination. Fr. Bernie had me enter what is known in the Exercises as "The Second Week" where Jesus is on earth and beginning his ministry. The first experience of Christ's ministry was his Baptism by John the Baptist in the River Jordan.

As I entered the scene (in my imagination) I was unable to move past this experience: I saw myself on the banks of the Jordan River, sitting on what seemed like a sandy and steep slope that fell toward the river. Each day I would sit quietly and imagine the scene. It was always the same! I saw two men in the water. One 'dunked' the other into the water and raised him up out of the water. I did not see or experience the private blessing Jesus and John heard on that day: "This is my beloved Son..."

By Thursday of that week, I was becoming frustrated and fatigued with this exercise. After about 20 minutes sitting by myself in the living room imagining this scene I spoke out loudly in a kind of rebellious moment: "What's the big deal! One guy dunks another guy in the water. I don't get it!"

Almost immediately I felt guilty about my outburst. I'm in prayer and I'm challenging the Scripture? If I don't get it, whose fault is that? God's or mine? So, I prayed: "Please forgive my impatience, Father. I know there is something in the Scripture reading you want me to experience, but I don't seem to be able to open myself to it. Please give me the grace to understand what it is you want me to hear from this reading."

I quieted myself and returned to the scene. Only this time I was not on the bank of the River Jordan looking at two men far away going through a seemingly mysterious and ineffable ritual. This time I was in the water, chest deep, standing next to Jesus and John. They did not see me. They were involved in their experience and I was simply an invisible bystander. I noticed that, in my imagination, Jesus was taller than John. I also noticed how reluctant John seemed to continue the baptismal process with Jesus. I couldn't hear them as they discussed John's dissonance. The water was dark, but not dirty. Like many rivers, the sediment in the Jordan made it difficult to see to the bottom of the river.

Just then I felt a pressure pushing me on top of my head, as if I were being 'dunked' in the water by an invisible force. I imagined it was God who was pushing me underwater, so I didn't resist. I took a deep breath and accepted the immersion. But, the force was not letting me surface. The force continued to hold me under water. So I waited...and I waited... and I waited!

"Is God trying to drown me?" I wondered to myself. Whatever happens in that imaginative time, one does not remove one's self from the scene when it gets scary.

Eventually, I could no longer hold my breath, even though I was still 'under water' in my imagination. "I'm going to experience drowning!" I concluded and I inhaled the water in which I was immersed.

I could breathe under water! I could breathe the very water that would normally fill my lungs with a substance I could not tolerate and live! The pressure on my head was removed but I did not rise from the water. I swam around like an otter! I saw the feet of Jesus and John. I could see and touch rocks, watch the sediments and fish float by as I swam around totally free in this amazing world in which I should not be able to live. I don't remember how long I stayed below the surface of the water. Was it seconds, five minutes, or twenty minutes? The length of time was irrelevant. What I experienced was relevant. It was truly a revelation from God.

What is clear to me, however, is that God made real for me the experience of life that continues after we are no longer dependent on meeting the physical needs that keep us alive. In Isaiah 43:1-2, there is a puzzling verse that has been clarified by this mysterious and gracious revelation. The verse explains, "Do not fear, for I have redeemed you; I have summoned you by name; you are mine. When you pass through the waters, I will be with you; and when you pass through the rivers, they will not sweep over you. When you walk through the fire, you will not be burned; the flames will not set you ablaze."

Through that revelation, and through my prayer life that continues to this day, I am no longer afraid of death. I will live forever in the Kingdom of God. I experienced a metaphorical death in the River Jordan and passed from this life in the flesh into a life of joy and freedom in my life in the Spirit.

My bone marrow disease blossomed into full blown acute myeloid leukemia during the winter of 2008. By February of 2009, I entered University of Michigan's Hospital and was there until the first of June. During that time it was touch and go. Eventually the doctors were successful in bringing my leukemia into remission. Then I received a bone marrow transplant. My brother, Mike, was a perfect match. Five years later I am still cancer free.

Being healed from leukemia gets people's attention. What I want you to know is that the more important healing was the one I received when God healed me of my fear of death. I was able to say, during that long and sometimes scary hospital stay: "Your will, Father. Whatever you decide will be your will and I am confident in your grace." Don't get me wrong. I didn't want to die. I wanted to live, and I told God that truth.

The Spirit Whispered: Do not be afraid. I've always got you. Live in freedom and love, and tell others how I saved you.

Prayer: Divine Spirit, you are always there for us if we call upon you. Help me never to take anything for granted. Your love and healing is unbelievable.

Rick Benedict, Professor Emeritus
Madonna University College of Education
Spiritual Director
Bloomfield Hills, MI

Whisper Thirty-One: Two Powerful Whispers

When I was in the hospital right after delivering my third baby, I had the most amazing experience. Our baby wasn't breathing correctly so my husband and the nurses took the baby out of the room right away to see what the problem was.

I was exhausted and scared that there was something wrong with our baby as I prayed to God to please help us. At some point, I fell asleep and was awakened to the most beautiful, calming and trusting man's voice I have ever heard saying, "Jasper." As I looked around the room to see who was speaking, I realized I was the only person there.

Moments later my husband was wheeling our baby back into the room and I told him what had just happened. He knew by the conviction in my voice that I thought I must have had some kind of spiritual experience. We had come to the hospital without a name for our son and I felt that we were to name our baby Jasper. We both were stunned as we spoke about this incredible spiritual experience.

Suddenly our baby started choking again. As they wheeled him back down the hallway again for more medical attention, the exact same thing happened to me. This time the spirit spoke the word, "Angel."

We left the hospital the next day with a perfectly healthy baby boy. We had decided to wait to name him until we could research the name Jasper and its meaning. We soon realized that it was a form of "Gaspar" who some believe was one of the Three Wise Men; his name meant "bearer of gifts." Without question, we knew we had just named our son "Jasper Angel."

Another powerful whisper happened years later. My dad was in the end stages of cancer. I decided that I would go to church and pray for my dad. That Monday, I stopped at a church that I had never been to before and attended noon mass at St. John Student Center.

When the priest, Fr Jake Foglio, requested that we state our intentions for others, I said, "Please pray that my dad goes peacefully to heaven. It is so hard to see him suffer."

After I spoke, this beautiful woman sitting in front of me turned around, touched my arm and said to me," I will pray for you, please wait after Mass for me."

When she touched me, I felt a peace which I had never experienced before and then I felt a rush of energy surge through my body. The message I received was, "You need to get to know her." After Mass I introduced myself to Sr. Dorothy and asked her to pray for my dad.

Over the next month, I continued going to that same parish for noon mass. As I got to know Sister Dorothy, we both felt we were destined to meet for many reasons. It felt like we had known each other for a long time as we were so comfortable spending time and sharing stories together.

A few weeks later, a friend of mine, Pam suggested that I go to my first confession before Mass. As I walked out of confession, I saw Pam and Sr. Dorothy sitting outside the door waiting for noon Mass to begin. After I shared my first experience with confession, I asked Sr. Dorothy to please pray for my dad. I specifically asked her to talk to Jesus [we learned she refers to Jesus as her "husband"], to take my dad home, so he wouldn't have to suffer anymore. That was about 12:05 p.m. When I left Mass and turned my phone on, there was a text message waiting for me saying that my dad had passed away at 12:11 p.m. Once again I felt the Spirit as a feeling of peace came over me, assuring me that my dad was at peace. I felt much better knowing that he wasn't suffering anymore. I truly believe that I had experienced a miracle. Words couldn't explain what had happened, but I knew my dad was with God and that I didn't have to worry anymore.

The Spirit Whispered: I know your needs before you speak them. Trust that I will always be there for you.

Prayer: Divine Spirit, you are always there to help me when I need you. Give me the wisdom and understanding that I need to put my trust in you at all times. Your love is healing. May I continue to be open to your promptings.

Kelle Donnelly Miller
Professional Photographer
Okemos, MI

―――――― ♦ ――――――

*"Happiness is the experience
of living every moment
with love, grace and gratitude."*

Denis Waitley

―――――― ♦ ――――――

Whisper Thirty-Two: Precious Twins

My husband and I were approaching the age of 30 and were sitting on our couch discussing our lives together (already 12 years at this point). We were laughing at so many great memories from graduations, our wedding weekend, and trips with college friends. We looked at each other and both knew it was probably time to close this chapter of our lives with just the two of us and open the next chapter with some little ones. We agreed there was no time table on having children, when it happened it happened. Later that year just before heading on a family vacation to San Diego, I was a little late and as I had a doctor's appointment scheduled, I figured I would have a pregnancy test done while I was there. The test came back negative, however, while on vacation something felt a little different than normal and I was still late.

When we got back home to Florida, I took a couple of home pregnancy tests and to our surprise, they were very positive. As any parent knows, this moment is an unexplainable combination of emotions, where one chapter in your life has turned and another is coming at you so fast, whether you are ready or not. We were somehow able to keep our news a secret for a couple of weeks until our family was together for Christmas. It was a very joyous and memorable holiday season, we were on cloud nine!

At our first ultrasound everything was great! The baby's heart beat was good, I was healthy, and there were no foreseeable problems. I was curious about one thing though, could I be having twins? My father-in-law is a fraternal twin, so I asked. The doctor gave us a quick biology lesson on twins: basically my husband's genes, in regards to *me* having twins, would not play a role. With fraternal twins the *mother* has to carry the gene to lay, if you will, more than one egg. At that point the eggs are fertilized by more than one sperm. The end result is multiple children with completely different sets of genes. This was the end of the conversation, one heart beat was heard, and we were beyond happy as we went along on our joyous day!

The next month, at 16 weeks gestation, we went in for our visual ultrasound to see our little one for the first time. My mom, aunt, husband, and I (I am Latin, so yes it is completely normal to have this many people with you for the ultrasound; if my grandma didn't live in South America, she would've been there too) were staring at the screen with anticipation, and all of a sudden the technician moved across my belly and there were the tops of not one, but two little heads! We all screamed for joy and surprise as we learned that we were having twin girls. My husband almost passed out as he mumbled; "Two proms, two weddings." Soon after, we were all swept up to another room to have a consultation with our neonatologist about how to proceed.

Our jubilation quickly turned into panic as he proceeded to tell us that one of our twins had a problem with the umbilical cord and could potentially be born with health issues, pass away during the pregnancy, or worse kill her sister along with herself during pregnancy. He believed that our children were living in a womb with cord insertion complications, or Twin-to-Twin Transfusion. When we had asked the doctor what he would do if he were in our shoes, he said "abort" and "start over again." We were shell shocked! This is a gut wrenching feeling that I would not want another person to experience. We did what any other parent would do at that time, research! We combed through every Internet resource and talked to any friends with past experiences that could help us with our decision. We had gone to another ultrasound thereafter and our baby "B" was growing, but at a slower rate than her baby "A" sister. We had a decision to make and were running out of time; this literally was a life or death situation!

When facing a life altering decision, you look for any help you can get. Prayers from friends, advice from family, and some answers from above, however, at the end of the day you have to trust yourself. This was our burden to bear, and we would have to live with our decision the rest of our lives. We decided to go with our gut and follow the natural path that was selected for us and go ahead with the pregnancy as is. We would go twice a month to have an ultrasound to monitor the progress. Baby "B" was still a little smaller but was growing. One day, at about 30 weeks, I felt faint and started having contractions. We went to the hospital. It turned out to be false labor pains; however, it opened our eyes and reminded us that we were not out of the woods yet.

At 34 weeks and a day, I woke up in the middle of the night with contractions. I woke up my husband and my mom, who just happened to be staying the night with us. We drove off to the hospital and somewhere between elevators C and D my water broke. It was time! A "C" section was scheduled due to the high risk. It was a little after 7:00 a.m. baby "A" was delivered and started crying. One minute later, baby "B" was delivered but there was no sound! After a couple of frantic seconds of doctors and nurses shuffling and shouting, we heard a cough and then a little cry. These two beautiful girls, Lydia Mara and Ella Sophia, were identical twin sisters (which we later came to realize are mirror image, identical twins: Lydia is left-handed and Ella is right-handed, amongst other mirror traits.) This is what the OBGYN had left out of our "twin" conversation: any woman can have *identical twins*. Identical twins are not genetic, it is when one fertilized egg splits into two separate, genetically identical embryos.

After ten days in the Neonatal Intensive Care Unit, we brought Lydia, baby A, home. Ten days later we brought Ella, our baby B, home. She was healthy and had no further complications. Life is so good!

The Spirit Whispered: Never give up, always trust yourself and believe in me. Your love for each other and the strength of your family will get you through this.

Prayer: Divine Spirit, we thank you for giving us the faith we needed to stay positive and believe that everything would work out. We have both been blessed by our beautiful girls. They are the joy of our life and both remain very healthy. We will continue to trust in you and never doubt your love for us.

Daniela and Matt Kaskey
Daniela, Vice President of Wolverine Engineering
Matt, Owner of "Catering by Matthew"
Sarasota, FL

Whisper Thirty-Three: My Son the Caddy

My wife always encouraged me to take my golf game seriously. The last 25-30 years, I only played about 10-15 times a year, but I always shot in the 80s. Sometimes I shot that elusive 70s score. My friends always encouraged me to play more, but I was busy coaching the local junior high football program and raising three sons. There was no time for golf. Well, the boys grew up, and when our last son went off to college, I started playing more. When I started working at my game, I found myself playing to a four handicap, so I decided to enter some senior amateur tournaments.

Three months before the Illinois State Amateur Qualifier, I discovered I had stage four throat cancer. I had the lump removed and my tonsils out. I had started chemotherapy, but decided to play anyway. I did not want to give in to the cancer. I was really struggling, not just because it was my first competitive golf competition but also because I was having the shakes from my chemo. The worst was yet to come. I had to undergo 24/7 chemo five days a week every other week, plus two radiation treatments a day. I could not eat or drink anything for three months; I received all my nourishment through a feeding tube. I lost almost 40 pounds.

I spent a lot of time in prayer. I was praying for all of those who were praying for me. I figured there was strength in numbers, and I wanted them to keep praying. I set a goal for myself. I decided I would play in the Chicago Golf District Senior Match Play qualifier in May. My treatments were to end two weeks before Christmas, and my feeding tube was scheduled to come out sometime in February. The cancer team thought this was rather humorous, but, with my feeding tube still in, I began hitting golf balls indoors in January. I had my feeding tube removed a month early, and forced myself to eat and work out. I didn't just want to play, I wanted to compete. I prayed to: St Jude, St Blaze, Our Blessed Mother and of course, Our Lord for just one good day in the sun. I knew I had lost some distance and strength capabilities and I was still about 20 to 25 pounds underweight, but my game seemed sound. My son, who was home from college and football practice for the spring, caddied for me.

We were blessed with a beautiful day, and after a birdie on the tenth hole, I was only two over par. A six over par would qualify me for the sixteen man match play. The back nine at the Elgin Country Club is very hilly, and the pace of play was very slow. Fatigue set in, and I ran out of gas. In retrospect, I should have used a cart, but I believe golf was made for walking if one is able. I was ten over par coming in to the 18th hole, and was out of contention. I pulled my drive on the 18th hole badly. I had to lay up—leaving me with a very tricky pitch which went 15 feet behind the hole, and I had a very fast downhill right to left putt.

I was the coach of the football team that my son, Bobby, had been on as an eighth grader. As I lined up the putt, he reminded me of what I always told him. As I crouched down to look the putt over, he calmly put a hand on my shoulder and said, "Pops, I know how disappointed you are, but you always taught us to play every play like it was the last of our life, to never give up. Now I am telling you, about two feet to the right, you can make this putt." The student was teaching the teacher, and that putt rolled right into the center of the cup. My playing partners were near tears as Bobby hugged me and told me how proud he was of me. The traditional handshakes from my buddies turned into hugs.

I don't believe in coincidences. All this happened for a reason. As I prepare for my tournament qualifiers this year, I know that I will be calmer and more grateful for just the thrill of playing the game rather than whether I qualify or not. God gave me a second chance, and sometimes it is good to have your words thrown back at you.

The Spirit Whispered: I gave you a second chance; now use the abilities that I gave you. Practice hard, and do your best to succeed, but never forget that success is secondary. Play every shot like I am watching you, and never lose faith.

Prayer: Divine Spirit, I know you will never leave me. You have always been there for me and for my family. You gave me a second chance. My faith in you continues to deepen. I know you will always be there for me. I trust in you and will never let you down.

Tom Purvin,
Aerospace Marketing Executive
Palatine, IL.

---•---

"We must make the world a place
where: love dominates our hearts,
nature sets the standard for beauty,
simplicity and honesty
are the essence
of our relationships,
kindness guides our actions
and everyone respects one another."

Susan Polis Schultz

---•---

Whisper Thirty-Four: Hearing God's Voice as a Teenager

There are a lot of things that influence you when you are a 15 year-old teenager: girls, peer pressure, teammates, classmates, pop culture and girls. It all seems so convincing and overwhelming when you're 15. At 15, the world revolves around your desires and your needs. At 15, your entire life's worth and happiness hinges on whether: you have the cool shoes, the nice jacket and the right haircut; on whether or not you'll be able to go the party, see this movie or go on that trip. Fifteen is a hard age, but that's exactly when I heard God's voice. In the midst of all that near-sightedness, narcissism and naïveté, God chose to speak to me. I think he knew that I had lots of other "voices" speaking to me so he made sure to speak to me in a way that I could clearly hear him.

I was at a church service not paying attention to anything going on, completely focused on, you guessed it, a girl. If I remember correctly, we were passing notes among friends and laughing about something. All of a sudden, I heard through the sound system speakers: "You, right there, young man, stand up." Frozen in horror I tilted my head to the right, the minister was standing at the end of my aisle pointing at me. I was mortified. I thought, "Well, there goes my weekend, I'm grounded." I also thought I'd be forever en-shrined in church history as one of those "disrespectful teenagers" that got called out during the sermon. The minister had crept up to our row with the wireless microphone; I was sure she had had enough of our talking and laughing and came over to make an example of us in front of 700 people. I slowly stood, expecting to be told I needed to pay attention to the message and stop causing trouble, but what happened next took me by surprise and changed my life.

God spoke to me. I didn't know it then but later it all made sense. The minister had a fierce look in her eye. She had her pointer finger pointing at me. She said:

> "Young man God has his hand on you. I don't know what your plans are after high school as far as education, but God has something for you, an oppor-

tunity, and you need to rethink your plans. His hand is on your life."

Then she went right back to delivering her message. That was it. That was all she said. I sat down and looked around at my friends in amazement and relief. I didn't quite know what to make of her message to me. The rest of the night I was so relieved that we didn't get in trouble and I thought of that more than anything else. But after that I was amazed that God chose to speak to a 15 year-old kid who wasn't even paying attention. In addition to the message God gave me that night, I learned a great lesson about mercy and grace. I deserved a good scolding from the minister and a kick in the pants for my inattentiveness and disruptive talking. Not only were those consequences suspended (mercy), but God chose to speak a message to her and she chose to obey his voice and deliver it to me (grace).

About six months after that encounter, I was in line at the airport leaving Grenada, a West Indian island nation. We had just spent 10 days doing mission work on the island with a missionary and his wife. While in line at the ticket counter in that small airport, Charlie, the missionary came up to me and said he had an offer for me: "I don't know how you feel about postponing your college plans, but we really could use you as an intern down here for a year."

As I spent the next 12 hours on planes and in airports, all I could think about was the minister's message to me six months earlier and what the missionary had just said. In my heart, I knew this was the opportunity she had mentioned in her message to me from God. I began to believe that God had a plan for me. He had a call for me to answer. And in his fatherly and loving way, he presented this call to me enough times so that I would know that he was calling me and what he was calling me to do.

On June 6, 2001, about 12 months after Charlie asked me to join his team, I boarded a plane to Grenada. I was 17 and had just graduated from high school two weeks earlier. A one year internship turned into a two year internship which then turned into a 13 year (and counting) relationship between me and the island of

Grenada. I moved back to New York City and went to college after two years in Grenada. But I've returned to Grenada seven times since I left in 2003, bringing dozens of others to experience the beauty of Grenada and minister God's love to his people.

The Spirit Whispered: Sometimes God whispers...sometimes he throws up a neon flashing sign so that not only 15 year-olds but all are aware and can't miss it.

Prayer: Divine Spirit, silence the other voices in my head so that I hear your voice clearly. Help me so that when I hear your voice, I will follow where you lead me.

Gabe Tringale, Worship and Media Pastor
Risen King Alliance Church
New York, NY

———•———

*"Let your heart guide you.
It whispers,
so listen carefully."*

———•———

Stu Krieger

Whisper Thirty-Five: The Rippling Effect of the Spirit

The Holy Spirit whispered to me,
"Ask for prayers. It's okay to ask for prayers."

But could I? After all, these wonderful spirit-filled people, who received numerous prayer requests sent out daily by a gracious soul (my friend Ed), were really strangers to me. I didn't know how many prayer warriors were on the distribution list ready to tackle my prayer, nor did I know who they all were. Somehow it didn't matter that through the years I had submitted prayer requests for others. I had even responded to several requests with personal notes and ways to help meet the person's needs. It just felt different being on the receiving end. The gentle, yet powerful Spirit kept nudging me until I quickly wrote:

Please pray for me and the quadruplets (a singleton and identical triplets) that I'm carrying. Each of their precious heart beats are dwindling by the day, just like the miscarriage I had suffered previously. They need to stay strong in order to survive.   *Many thanks, Donna*

As I exhaled, I pressed the send button. Okay, I told myself, now the world knows I'm early on in my pregnancy and need a miracle. But rather than feel uneasy, I felt at peace knowing my prayers, along with those of my husband of 11 years, were being supported by an army of people uniting their prayers with ours. Soon people were e-mailing notes, telling us how touched they were by our plight and were storming heaven.

Although, I truly believe each prayer was heard, God didn't answer in the way we all had hoped. The day after Mother's Day, we received confirmation that all their heart beats eventually stopped, without any known reason. Unbeknownst to me, the Holy Spirit was prompting numerous souls from the prayer list to reach out in support and comfort by various means, which truly touched our hearts.

Sitting across the bridge in Rockland County, the Holy Spirit was prompting yet another person to take action. This time, the Spirit was whispering to Joanne who my husband and I met several years ago on a retreat, but hadn't seen or heard from since. Joanne's e-mail invited us to a Mass of Healing and Remembrance that honors the memory of children who had been lost through miscarriage, stillbirth or infant death. It sounded nice, but since it was a work week and a long trek from our home to New Jersey to attend the evening service, we graciously declined. It wasn't until after Joanne's gentle persistence that we decided at the last minute to attend.

Like us, Joanne drove a long distance in order to meet us at the beautiful, stone Church of the Presentation. During the service, which was unlike anything we had ever experienced, Joanne held my hand, offered tissues on a continuous basis and walked along side us as we were instructed to go outside to the field for the balloon lift. Everyone in attendance was asked to write the name of the child they wanted to honor on a balloon. The quadruplets, plus our previous miscarriage totaled five names that we placed on three balloons. As I handed one of the balloons to Joanne, while my husband and I each held onto one, she was pleasantly taken by surprise. We told her it would mean so much to us if she would release the balloon with us. On the count of three, everyone on the field released their balloon, while Celine Dion's song "Fly" filled the spring, evening air. Everyone watched in amazement as the scattered balloons miraculously flocked together, gracefully drifting overhead lifting some of the heavy grief every parent felt. Looking up to the sky, everyone in attendance stood in complete awe without uttering a word. Joanne then revealed that the Holy Spirit led her to tell us about this special service, and how she hoped it would be the start of our healing journey. That night, which will forever be etched in our hearts, was truly the start of our healing and our deep gratitude to Joanne.

Four months later, we received devastating news; Joanne had been diagnosed with stage four inflammatory breast cancer. We were now the ones who were trying our best to comfort and support her during her brutal battle. One year and eight months later from

132

when we attended the Healing and Remembrance Mass, I was back at the big, stone church in New Jersey. It was so surreal for me, since this time I was there for Joanne's funeral. Unlike last time, I didn't have Joanne to comfort me nor offer me tissues as the tears rolled down my face. Instead of Joanne holding my hand, my five month-year-old baby was tightly holding onto me, as I grieved the loss of my dear friend who was only 48 years of age. As my sweet baby boy put his face to mine and smiled, it became clear to me at that moment. One of Joanne's last missions on earth was to help us heal. I will be forever grateful that Joanne listened to the Holy Spirit, and that I listened as well.

A month after her burial, Joanne's sister wrote this to me,

> *"Joanne was definitely guided by the Holy Spirit. She had told me about the prayer and remembrance service you attended and how moved she was when you turned and handed her Rose Lynn's balloon. I don't think she realized before then, that she also needed this kind of healing since she had never had a child; it was definitely something she expected to have in her life once she was married. For whatever reason, it wasn't to be, so you handing her that balloon was significant for Joanne as it allowed her to somehow grieve her own loss. Thank you for that. No doubt, that was another deed generated by the Holy Spirit."*

The Spirit Whispered: Your lives are all intertwined, and when you allow me to guide you, there is a rippling effect on all those who hear and act on my message.

Prayer: Divine Spirit, please open every person's heart to hear when you whisper, and to have courage to take action. An act of kindness may heal a soul in ways one may never know.

Donna DiMaio Rooney
Freelance publicist, working in the TV industry, published author
Connecticut

"... When the whole soul is yielded to the Holy Spirit, God Himself will fill it. "

Andrew Murray

Whisper Thirty-Six: An Unqualified Calling

God definitely has a sense of humor; otherwise he wouldn't have used a person like me to share his love with the world.

It all started in a little college town in Northern California where a lost, tequila-drinking college girl searched desperately for acceptance—in things like fraternity guys and keg parties—and came up empty.

No one had ever spoken to her about God except maybe her mom, whose limited understanding led her to share simply that God was like a force...as in Star Wars. That conversation and one with a born-again first-grade teacher, who had a conversion experience after receiving a cancer diagnosis, left the girl confused without an understanding of God. In fact, her first grade teacher had insisted that she believe in God. But it just didn't make sense to a six-year-old mind; Mrs. C had gone from being a funky belly-dancer to an uptight evangelical Christian who told the little girl that dancing was Satan's work. Her child's mind pictured little black devils with horns and pitchforks dancing in circles. The girl made up her mind right then to forget about believing in God.

And yet, God pursued a relationship with that child and at the age of 23, he showed up...literally and silently. And there was no denying that he was something way greater than she could have ever imagined.

That little girl is me and although I had little interest in him, he showed up one night in the form of an 8-foot, exceedingly bright white light in the shape of a cross on my neighbor's wall. He was there, quite real and yet I didn't know what to make of this incredible vision. He compelled me gently and silently to sit in his presence. Something happened that night and I was changed inwardly.

Outwardly, I continued to drink although not as a destructively. In fact, for the last year, things were mostly calm albeit depressing (alcohol acts like a depressant for the alcoholic) until I finally cried out to God and asked for help. He answered in the form of a magazine article about "grace in recovery." And with that, my journey to him really began.

My newfound fellow recovering drunk friends spoke of a "Group of Drunks" or the "Great Outdoors" as acronyms for God. At first, God was just a three-letter word and something that I would pray to while looking at the ceiling, hoping against hope that he would answer my prayers. And he did. One time I asked for help because the waitress who was training me at the fancy Italian restaurant, wouldn't stop talking about the end of the shift when we could taste every wine in the place. He answered by having her forget all about tasting wine and she just went home at the end of her shift. Another time I asked God whether or not I was supposed to date the cute guy that wanted to find out more about sobriety. I had my answer when the guy didn't show up at the meeting where we had plans to meet. And one day at a time, he kept me from picking up a bottle of tequila or even a glass of wine.

I searched continually for a greater relationship with this new God that I had found: new age churches where anything goes, Eastern meditation that seemed to focus on feeling good, Hindu groups that felt good but seemed to have limited truth, and hiking the valleys of Yosemite National Park. All were momentarily wonderful, but I knew intuitively that there was more. Each thing seemed like a broken arrow that was trying desperately to point to the truth. There were elements of good in each, but nothing stuck. I kept looking.

In the midst of my quest, I heard his voice. "Call FM102 (a local top forty radio station) and volunteer to be an intern." This message was unmistakably clear and commanding. I followed his direction and a door opened for a career in radio broadcasting. This path would include hip-hop, country and eventually contemporary Christian music. But first, I would have to surrender my pagan gods and encounter the One True God.

Pain can make you desperate. After a few years into belt buckles, rodeos and a life in country music radio, my life started to look like a country song: my boyfriend left in the middle of the night with no

136

forwarding address, one of my dogs died of inoperable cancer and I had just enough cash for a McDonald's hamburger. My mind suddenly opened and this time when I cried out to God, I heard something new.

"Stay close to me. Be obedient. Listen to my voice." Obedient? That word was not even in my vocabulary. The concept of obedience had been limited to dogs and training. These had to be God's instructions.

Not long after this close encounter with the Creator of the Universe, a friend showed up at my house with a bag lunch, some Christian tapes and a completely new and different outlook on life. She had transformed from a completely self-centered, vain woman of loose morals to the woman who presently stood in front of me—a soft-spoken, kind, thoughtful, grace-filled woman. Something or someone had gotten to her.

"I've gone back to church."

So that was it. Good for her. My broken heart and crushed ego were eager for the Truth. As I drove to work, I listened to the tapes which spoke of thanking God for everything—good and bad. As I praised him, the Spirit led me right to my friend's unbelievably beautiful, spirit-filled four square church on the questionable side of town. It didn't matter—driving to Compton would have been worth it for the sense of joy that I found. Nothing could keep me from Jesus and I'd found heaven on earth.

For the next few years, Jesus watered my soul. His love poured over me and through me and washed out all of the junk and shame that I had carried for so long. The change wasn't instant, but it was profound. I wanted to tell everybody about Jesus. And I did.

After ten years in radio, God led me to a little Christian radio station in northern California and it was there that he really began to speak to me.

"Trust me. Focus only on me. Let me guide you." Praying on the air became the norm and listeners would often tell me that it was their favorite part of the broadcast. We would regularly thank God for answered prayer requests as we would receive them and it became commonplace to hear of cancer disappearing, marriages restored and prodigal children returning home. Miracles became so common-place that it was actually strange when something went the opposite way. (Of course, God is sovereign and his will is beyond my understanding.)

After seven years, I thought that I was done with radio. I had miraculously gotten pregnant at the advanced age of 41 and planned to stay home forever and raise my son. My husband sup-ported my decision until the day his prosperous business completely dried up and then he begged me to go back to work. I knew that if I applied to various radio stations that there was a good chance I would find work. God gave me clear direction once again.

"Check KLOVE's website." I felt like Jonah. God had called me to work at this monstrously huge Christian radio network several times before and I blew off the idea. I knew that God was calling me again to work for his outlet for the Gospel.

Miraculously, KLOVE allowed me to work and broadcast from home for the next two years. When it was time to honor my commitment to move to the area closer to the station headquarters, God reminded me to praise him for the land that he would provide for us. And he did there were 20 other bidders on our little house and ours was the bid accepted.

The folks listening to the 2:00-5:00 a.m. CST shift are usually night owls—cops, nursing moms, ER nurses and folks battling with all sorts of demons. I prayed regularly, shared about Jesus and tried to remind people that God loved them. Occasionally, I would try to be topical and mention various news stories or weight loss tips. It was during those times that God let me know exactly what he wanted me to talk about to his children.

I received it as a reminder that God is eternal and that as one of his servants in the media, my job was to stay true to my calling—to speak of his glory and not the world's.

God has been faithful to me, my family and to the ministry of KLOVE. I believe it is his desire to be honored in his own house and to encourage his children all over the world with constant reminders of his unfailing love and unchanging mercy.

The story is not over yet and with his grace, it will continue to unfold into something beautiful.

The Spirit Whispered: Trust me. Rely on me. I love you. I see you and I want to be near you. Share my love with others and draw near to me. Do not be afraid. My grace is sufficient in your weakness. I will answer when you call. I'm never far away.

Prayer: Divine Spirit, we are so grateful for your presence. Thank you Jesus for being close and loving us. Continue to guide us and lead us into the way everlasting.

Monika Kelly, on-air personality, at KLOVE
a national Christian radio network
Sacramento, CA

―――――― • ――――――

*"Your best friend
is the person
who brings out the best
that is within you."*

Henry Ford

―――――― • ――――――

Whisper Thirty-Seven: On This Path to God

I celebrate the mystery of life and the many experiences encountered on this path to God.

At the age of 14, I was guided to Christ the King Church in San Diego, CA. It was there that I noticed a bass guitar on a stand not being played by anyone during a music rehearsal for *Folk Mass*. My brother Ray was singing and my brother David was playing guitar along with some other local musicians. The Spirit whispered *pick up the bass,* so after making sure it was okay, I picked it up and immediately started to play along with everyone. The Spirit must have been whispering which notes to play as well, because without any prior experience whatsoever, I was able to keep up with the music. I also discovered some magical notes to play that led to an invitation to be part of the band. Just like that, in a moment, my life changed and it would never be the same again. Little did I know that not only had I just discovered my future occupation, but the bass guitar would be my ticket to a life that I never could have imagined in a million years. I would later travel the world performing with a diverse array of artists including: Eric Clapton, Barry White, George Harrison, Quincy Jones, Phil Collins, Al Jarreau and many more. I would make records with: Michael Jackson, Barbara Streisand, Stevie Wonder, Bob Dylan, Aretha Franklin and Whitney Houston to name just a few. All of this as a result of picking up that bass guitar in Christ the King Church!

My brother Ray was ordained a priest shortly after and now *Monsignor* Raymond East leads the Parish at St. Teresa of Avila Catholic Church in Washington, D.C. David still plays the guitar and resides with his family in Colorado. More than forty-five years later, I am still doing one of the things that I love doing the most, and that is playing the bass. In 2014, I released my very first solo album and to this day, the Spirit whispers to me which notes to play.

My belief is that the Spirit whispers to us from the day we are born. Actually, before we are born or how else would our hearts know how to beat, and how would we learn to breathe unless we were guided by the Spirit? But how does it speak to us? With so much noise around these days I find that I have to go to a very quiet space to hear the Spirit whisper. I am able to find that space through prayer and meditation which allows me to listen not only with my ears but also with every fabric of my being. Since the Spirit is all around us, we don't have to wait until we are in a space of silence, we are being whispered to at every intersection, at every turn. I think it is important to be tuned in to the Spirit and simply be aware. Much like pilots dial in a frequency to hear the flight instructions from the control tower, by tuning into the Spirit, we are guided at every turn.

The Spirit Whispered: I saw the look in your eye when you first spotted the bass guitar. I knew you had the gift to play it, and I knew you would bring more people to God by using your gift. I am proud of you because you listened. Continue to share your gift, you have been blessed.

Prayer: Divine Spirit, I am grateful for your guidance throughout my life. You have graciously blessed me with a gift that will draw others to you. Help me to live by your word, and make me an instrument of your peace. Bless all of the children who are searching to use their gifts and talents. Guide us, protect us and help us become a blessing to one another.

Nathan East, Grammy nominated bassist,
songwriter and recording artist
in jazz, rhythm and blues
rock and pop music
Los Angeles, CA

Whisper Thirty-Eight: What A Friend!

I was born to two wonderful parents in the beautiful island of Trinidad. At eighteen months old, my parents decided to move to the United States to further their education and provide better opportunities for our family. My mom was a nurse and my dad a teacher. From my earliest recollection, there was always music in our home, and we had a piano. Dad would play that incredible instrument and amaze me. So much so, that at the age of four, my parents heard music coming from the piano. Curious as to who could be playing, they walked into the living room to find me playing an actual song, even though my feet couldn't reach the pedals. They watched in stunned silence, then mumbled some adult stuff and smiled. And so began my musical life at the piano.

Years later, my dad was called back to Trinidad and Tobago to finish building a Christian high school where he would serve as principal. One day while at school, we received a tragic call that our house was on fire. We were traumatized by the news, and immediately left the school in a rush to get to our home. I remember that the short ride to the house seemed like forever. All the way home, I was thinking about one thing, my piano. Not just any piano, but my piano; the one that had prepared me to become one of the main pianists at our church at the age of eight. The instrument I spent hours playing and where I learned classical pieces and hymns.

I didn't realize that at that tender age I was being divinely prepared for my life's vocation: a calling. When we arrived at the house, it was engulfed in flames. In minutes, everything was gone including my beloved piano. My brothers and I were crying, but not Dad. He took his fancy camera out of the car with a smile on his face, and to everyone's amazement started taking pictures. I watched him encourage people around him as he smiled and took pictures of our burning home. Some people might have thought he'd gone mad, but the look on his face was not one of denial, but of peace and faith. This was my first significant encounter with the Spirit. I watched my father shine at a time when he could have fallen apart. I watched him do this while others observed him and wondered what was wrong with him. What I witnessed that day became the spiritual inspiration that would last into my adult life and the spiritual fuel that would propel me along the path God had chosen for me.

Being called and choosing to answer the call to be a professional musician, whose mission is to change the world through music, hasn't been an easy journey. I've encountered many fires along this journey. And there were times that I felt as if the fire would consume everything important to me. Yet, in those times I heard the Spirit reminding me that I was called to be a minstrel, just as my father had been. And God has honored his promise to not allow the flames of life to overtake me (Isaiah 43:2). He has been there, leading me through the opened doors of success, and he has been there to reassure me on the days when I wanted to quit. He promised to be with me through adversity, through fire, through disappointment, through every season of my life like the most faithful of friends. I'm reminded of a hymn entitled, "What a Friend We Have in Jesus." It is such a meaningful message that I recorded a version of that hymn and called it "What a Friend." And, truly he is just that; a friend who bears all of our grief and who never leaves us.

The Spirit Whispered: I'm always with you. I will always be your unconditional friend. No matter what is happening in your life, trust in me and draw close to me.

Prayer: Divine Spirit, I'm amazed at your boundless capacity to love me through anything. Thank you for being my friend. The more I trust you the more I experience your love and support.

Roger Ryan, a Grammy, Dove nominated, and Juno Award winning music producer, his musical career is based on the theme: "Music Is For The SOUL"

Whisper Thirty-Nine: He Saved My Life

Two weeks ago, I felt myself getting weaker and weaker each day and by the end of the week I had the strangest feeling I was dying. I wasn't frightened but just disappointed that I had never prepared anybody for all the complicated things I have been involved in. Knowing that I had an appointment in two days with my cardiologist I decided to tell him what I was experiencing. He tested my blood and immediately sent me to my primary care doctor who took my blood again and tested it. By then my red blood cell count had dropped two more points. He sent me over to the emergency ward at St. Peter's Hospital where they took me right in, took my blood for another test and got a team of different doctors to find out where I was bleeding. Nobody could find any sign of internal bleeding from any of my organs.

At that point, a physician's assistant came into my hospital room and sat down and told me his name, Murtaza Singaporewala. He was a Shiite Muslim. He shared that he used to work for Borders Bookstore 20 years ago when JOSHUA became an international phenomenon. He had followed me ever since and was so happy he finally met me and that he could be of help to me. So, he took my blood and tested it. In ten minutes he found out what was wrong; my autoimmune system was destroying my red blood cells as they were being introduced into the blood stream. In two days, I would have no red blood cells, no oxygen and that could end my life.

He told the other doctors and the head of the hematology team, Dr. Qui Zen, what he found. Dr. Zen accepted his findings and immediately gave me 80 mgs of prednisone, and a blood transfusion, which my young godson, Peter Della Ratta recommended to boost the oxygen level. (Peter knew nothing about anemia prior to what he learned on the computer the night before.) The doctor did add the blood transfusion, and within one hour I felt like a new man. Hopefully, the doctors thought that within a month or so of this program, the problem should be ended and may never come back again.

While I was in the hospital, there was a young man in the bed next to me who was extremely sick and doctors from various major hospitals could not find the cause. He hadn't eaten in days and his family was beside themselves. I talked to him and we soon became friends. When he overheard the Muslim doctor talking with me the way he did and how my life was an adventure with Jesus, the young roommate was impressed.

He said to me, "I have learned a lot in the past two days. I finally realized that I have to find Jesus and become close to him. I learned a lot of other things, too."

I told him I learned a lot from him as well.

He said, "I think we must be soul mates."

The boy was a pre-med student. That afternoon his doctor came in and said he was going to prescribe a medicine that he thought might work. An hour later I went home, but before I left, I told him, "I think that you will be released tomorrow. I believe that Jesus arranged for us to meet and now that we have, there's no need for you to be here anymore."

He emailed me when I got home, and said how uncanny it was because he was going to be released the next day.

What I learned is that Jesus has a strange sense of humor as we both met as very sick patients in the same hospital room for the same three days. I guess the sicknesses were what brought us together initially, that and the right topics of conversations.

The second day I was there, the Muslim came to visit me again. While he was there visiting me, a dear friend, who is dying of Lou Gehrig's disease, came to see me at the same time. There in my room we had a Catholic priest, a Muslim and a Jew having fun over the beautiful experience. How delicately Jesus arranges even such small details!

I now owe my life to the brilliance of a Muslim doctor whom Jesus picked to help me! Also, when some people cynically ask, "Where are there any Muslim hospitals?" I can only answer, "One third of the doctors, nurses and assistants at St. Peter's and also around the country are Muslims. It appears that they would prefer work in Catholic hospitals rather than build their own."

The Spirit Whispered: I arranged this meeting for you. My Spirit is always with you wherever you go. I will see that you receive the care you need. When you are weary and weak, you need to take time to rest. Do not worry, trust in me. I will remain steadfast and never leave you. Whenever you are struggling or weary come to me and I will give you rest.

Prayer: Divine Spirit, I will continue to trust that you will always see that I am cared for when I am unable to care for myself. You have never left me and you have always healed what needs to be healed in me. I am grateful for your constant love.

Joseph F. Girzone
Priest and Author of *Joshua*
Altamont, NY

---◆---

"*Love is a partnership of
two unique people
who bring out the very best
in each other
and who know that even though
they are wonderful as individuals,
they even are better together.*"

Barbara Cage

---◆---

Whisper Forty: I'm Glad I Listened to My Intuition

In the late summer of 1977, I had begun working at McDonald's. The hours were not meant for a morning person! Each day, I would work either afternoons from noon to eight or four to close, which could be midnight or if there was cleanup, two a.m. The end of the closing shift included: emptying the daylong grease from the fryer, cleaning a bathroom for the sixth time that shift, washing every corner of the counter and its shelves below as well as filling every single bin! The full bins were extremely important to our fellow McDonald's co-workers who would greet the next day about 5:30 a.m.

During the closing shift, plans were often being made for after work. About 2:00 a.m. these hardworking teens, with a "ring around our heads" and flattened hair from our trendy uniform hats, would plan to go out. Some nights this would result in going to someone's house and playing cards. Sometimes the older workers headed to a bar and stayed until the early morning hours. As a high school student, I usually got picked up by my mom and went home. One evening when my shift was over, I called to get a ride home. As I stood asking one of my siblings to get mom because I needed a ride home, I heard a deep voice from the end of the room say, "I'll give you a ride".

I turned around and said, "No thank you." When my mom got to the phone, I said, "Mom, could you please come and get me? There is a strange guy who wants to give me a ride."

Shortly thereafter I was closing again and one of the "closers" (a term for those of us who closed down the restaurant) asked me if I would consider going out with her friend. She knew that he had a crush on me. Truthfully, the thought of having a guy interested in me was mind-blowing and scary.

As long I can remember, I have been belittled and abused by the men in my life. My grandfather began sexually abusing me when I was just two and a half years old until I was eighteen, followed by my favorite uncle (who told my father I needed a girdle in the third grade). My father would hit and threaten me, so that I would tell him where my mom and I had hidden the alcohol. Up to this point in my life I had only known pain from men, and while getting out of the house was a tremendous relief, dating had not even entered my mind. In fact, during my high school years, I seriously contemplated becoming a nun. This "calling" was simply a desperate search for safety and would not be a part of my journey, although my life has been a miraculous journey and filled with inspirational moments.

So, as we all cleaned the fryers, counters, floors, etc., my co-worker's friend would periodically walk near me. One of our fellow closers asked me what I was doing the next day as we were both scheduled off. I responded, "Probably nothing, as we only have one car and six drivers, so I can never go anywhere." During the entire evening I kept myself busy with my closing duties, while wrestling with the fact that though I was deathly afraid of dating, I really liked the attention from the young man.

It was during this period of time, as I was thinking that "I have no idea what to do" and "this guy will hurt me in some way," that I remember a strong whisper that I needed to say, "Yes." I hesitated and resisted but my gut feeling was that I should say yes—the whisper and wisdom of the Spirit knew that this was a special young man. I am extremely grateful that I listened to this whisper.

While there were many bumps, tears, counselors and personal transformations along the way, I want you to know that seven years later, I married that deep voiced, young man. Today we celebrated our 30th wedding anniversary. I know now that when I listen to the Spirit and trust, miracles happen.

The Spirit Whispered: Listen to me and trust me. I know what is good for you, and I will always be by your side. Ask for my help and guidance and then listen to your inner voice. I am trying to protect you and give you a wonderful life.

Prayer: Divine Spirit, I feel blessed that you continue to guide me and share your wisdom in my life. Help me to remain open and respond courageously to new ways to share my story and improve the lives of children across the country.

Suzanne Greenberg, President/CEO
Child Abuse and Neglect Council
Great Lakes Bay Region
Saginaw, MI

―――――― • ――――――

"When the world says,
'Give up,'
Hope whispers,
Try it one more time.'"

Hannah Miles

―――――― • ――――――

Whisper Forty-One: Why Do You Doubt Me?

When my children were young I taught them as much as I could about God, but the Holy Spirit was difficult to describe. Late one winter afternoon, as it was getting dark, we had a talk about God and how we know he works in our lives. Pointing to an electric outlet, I asked them what was in it. They said "electricity." I asked how they knew that and my youngest, Maryclare, replied that when you plug in a lamp it lights up. We then discussed how much help light is in our life. I told them that the Holy Spirit is like the electricity in the wall socket. It's always there to help but you have to plug into it. Then I turned off the lights. There was still some light outside but it was pretty dark in the house. I asked them if they would help me fix dinner, set the table and boil some water for macaroni and cheese...without the lights. After some stumbling and dropped silverware, we all agreed that having that bright light in the kitchen made doing our chores much easier. I told them that we can all stumble along in life without asking for the Holy Spirit's help, but everything is so much clearer with his light shining and helping us with everyday tasks and decisions.

Maryclare must have taken that lesson to heart. Years later, when she was pregnant with her little girl she was having trouble walking and doing her job as a physical therapist assistant. She was experiencing numbness in her left leg and her doctor assured her that the baby was pressing on her spine and after delivery everything would be just fine. She fell on the way to work one day toward the end of the pregnancy. Her doctor put her on bed rest for the last few weeks and decided to induce the baby for the safety of both mother and baby. After a long delivery, she was brought back to her room and her husband and I helped her to the bathroom. Her legs didn't seem to be working very well.

The next afternoon, I was in the room when a cheery young nurse said, "Time to get up and walk Mommy." My daughter replied that she couldn't walk. Then the cheery nurse said, "Oh, I know, it's painful but you need to move to keep your circulation going. Come on, I'll help you." I took my granddaughter and the nurse rolled the little baby crib next to the bed. Maryclare stiffened her legs and wobbled a few steps looking like Frankenstein with the bassinet for support. Then she stopped and asked the nurse for a chair before she fell down. The nurse got a chair. Maryclare rested and then her husband and the nurse helped her back into bed. Suddenly, the nurse acted very professional and left the room.

It wasn't long before seven doctors circled my daughter's bed and conferred about possible spinal cord injuries. They poked with pins and used little spiked wheels on her legs to determine what was happening. After an MRI we had our answer. Maryclare's spinal cord was being pinched by a disc at her spine's number eleven vertebra. All women's pelvic bones "loosen up" before delivery of a baby, but hers had extended up her spine and somehow, during the long delivery, a disc had slipped and crushed her spinal cord. They said they were sorry but this happens about once in every 2.7 million deliveries. The hospital gave her a wheelchair and sent her home.

When we got to their house, I wanted to make up a bed for her on the first floor. She wouldn't hear of it and army-crawled her way up stairs to her bedroom. This was just the beginning of her de-termined outlook on life. She had to be so careful when she turned over in bed because her legs would just keep going and she would end up on the floor. We got so we would laugh about her 'independent' legs. Her paralysis was from her ribcage down but she was sure that God didn't expect her to spend her life in a wheelchair. She scooted down the stairs in the mornings and went about her household tasks as best she could in the chair. And the whole time I was praying—praying, pleading, begging God to help her adjust to this new way of life. She was praying, too, but she was thanking God for each new little tingle of feeling or twinge of pain below her waist.

To my amazement, she asked the Holy Spirit to give her patience; the patience to be able to wait until she was healed and walking. She was absolutely sure that the Holy Spirit was going to heal her. Because she had worked in physical therapy, she knew exactly how bad her cord injury was and what the prognosis was. She believed that God would either heal her or give her the strength to handle this new life. She had a few home visits from a therapist before her job was terminated and her insurance stopped. The therapist kindly laid out a care plan for her to follow and left looking sad. I still remember the day she stood up from her wheelchair. She held onto a walker, and then let go of it to clap her hands. I cheered as if she had just scored a winning basket at the buzzer! She could stand and clap her hands! Hooray!

Maryclare had the baby in October and by mid-December I knew I had to go home and allow this family to work things out on their own. Two parishes near her home were helping out with shopping and meals. Maryclare was handling most of the cooking and cleaning and still dragging herself upstairs each night and scooting down each morning. I alerted both of her neighbors that if they should see the house on fire while her husband was at work, to go catch the baby while she crawled out the door. Since it was an older home, the wheelchair always got caught in the narrow doorframe to the side porch.

My husband and I visited them regularly. It was only an hour's drive and we loved seeing our new granddaughter. Maryclare didn't seem to be getting any better. I asked her how she was doing. She said that she had a lot of pain and decided to have a "pity party" but nobody came so she gave up on that idea. Instead she kept on praying for patience until she could walk again. She was seeing one of the spinal cord doctors who had been shaking his head at her bedside in the hospital. He was really exasperated and told her that she should wait longer between visits because he knew she was paying for her appointments out of her own pocket. He wasn't seeing much improvement and was discouraged.

Time passed and soon it was Easter Sunday. I had asked Maryclare and her husband to come for Easter dinner. She said she would think about it but she told me the ride in the car was bumpy and made her back hurt. I had just put the vegetables to simmer when I looked out the front window. Maryclare was walking with her walker up our front walk. It took her twenty-two minutes to walk from the truck up to the porch and into the house. I was bawling like a baby when she finally sank into her wheelchair to rest. She said she planned to be walking by the time the baby was walking. "We'll learn together!" she said with a grin.

In June, she had her last doctor's appointment. She was walking down the hall using a four-point cane when the doctor greeted her. He was astounded and said, "I can't believe this is the same young woman I saw in the hospital eight months ago!!!" Then he bellowed, "Who prescribed that four-point cane?" And she hollered back at him, "I DID! I was tripping over my dumb walker." She just grinned at him. During the visit, he gave her the DVD of her spinal MRI. Her cord had been 92% occluded by the disc. He said he held very little hope for her recovery when she was diagnosed. He just couldn't believe it. She laughed at him and said, "Well, DUH!!! I had about a thousand people praying for me between my parish here and my mom's parish back home!" He told her that he wasn't one of those praying kind of people but he might have to become one after this.

Life after her miracle wasn't all roses. They lost their home and had to come and live with us. (We love having our granddaughter in the house!) Their home had been closed up while waiting to sell and filled up with black mold after a flood in the basement. They lost everything and Maryclare really changed after that. She no longer cares about the things people have, she only cares about people. She says when you lose your stuff and can't walk, the Holy Spirit makes your priorities very plain. She still has pain but she says pain is much better than no feeling and no movement. She also has some paralysis issues that are scary, like when her diaphragm forgets how to work, but she just prays her way through them. I am still in awe at how God worked in my daughter's life and showed his love and compassion. And my Maryclare says, "I got a miracle. I am a walking testimony that he still works miracles on regular people. You just have to keep praying and thanking, the Holy Spirit will do the rest."

The Spirit Whispered: Why do you doubt me? I am the one in power, not you. I have always loved and taken care of you. All will be well.

Prayer: Divine Spirit, help me to understand that you are in charge and I only need to believe and be patient. All will be well.

Jeannie Lawrence
Co-Owner of "The Cakery" with Maryclare
Lansing, MI

―――――•●•―――――

*"Love's greatest gift is its ability
to make everything it touches
sacred."*

Barbara de Angelis

―――――•●•―――――

Whisper Forty-Two: Whispers and Shouts

The Spirit whispered to me in 1960 when I decided to enter the seminary, then again in 1963 when I realized it was time to leave. For the next two years, the Spirit's whispers at times became shouts. I didn't always hear let alone listen to them, but neither, thank God, did I completely ignore her relentless calls.

Years later, with the advantage of hindsight, I realized the compelling part of this journey began in the fall of 1963. After three years in seminary, I returned to Ohio's Kent State University. It was quite literally a last minute decision to finish my undergraduate education there instead of the East Coast. For most of the year I lived in a fraternity house over a mile's walk from campus, so the advantage of buying a meal pass on campus made sense. Besides, after three years of being "out of circulation," I wanted to be close to where I could best complete my transition from the routine of seminary life. The nearest eatery was the cafeteria in a women's dorm off Main Street. Little did I realize that it would set the stage for all that followed. During my first meal there, I met Paula. She was sitting with two girlfriends whom I knew casually and who, like her, had just transferred to Kent after two years at a private college. One of the women noticed and signaled for me to join them, two of them on one side of the booth, Paula and me on the other. My presence there that day, so early in the term, was purely coincidental. Or so it seemed at the time.

Our meal together was relaxing and congenial, but no audible bells rang, and I wasn't aware of any special chemistry between us—though admittedly I have always found science challenging. Years later, Paula told me—and her two friends confirmed—that the minute I left their booth, she confided to them, "I think that's the guy I'm going to marry."

During the next several months, in between seeing others, I asked her out. Horseback riding was not the best choice for our first date. Paula's steed ran off with her into a corn field, only to return much later and, as she dismounted, stepped on her foot. But neither mishap discouraged her or me. We continued to date intermit-

159

tently, even as I persisted in meeting other women. By mid-spring 1964, we were seeing each other exclusively.

After graduating late in the summer of 1964, I left Kent State for graduate school at Michigan State University intent on earning a Ph.D. Paula remained at Kent for her last year. We communicated through letters, phone calls and a few mutual visits. Then, on one of my weekends at Kent in late fall 1964, in the silence of an empty parish church, the Spirit shouted. I finally heard and proposed. The rest is "our story."

We married the following summer. Two years later, the Spirit showed with a flourish that she had been whispering to another couple as well. My younger brother married Paula's younger sister. Our children grew up together and we all remain close to this day. In August 2015, Paula and I will celebrate fifty years together. Only the Spirit knows how different our lives would have been had I decided not to return to Kent State in the fall of 1963. God knows I'm happy I did.

The Spirit Whispered: I am relentless. I will whisper, shout or do whatever it takes to help you to be where you need to be. I am the source and sustenance that will penetrate your crass or invincible resistance. I will remind you daily who is the source and sustenance of the better angels within us.

Prayer: Divine Spirit, you can whisper, cajole, shout. I am a hard-headed man. At times, you will have to pummel your way in. Be my guest.

Samuel J. Thomas, PhD, Professor Emeritus
Michigan State University, Department of History
East Lansing, MI

Whisper Forty-Three: Even While Sleeping

Because my daughter has Type One diabetes, I check her blood sugar level throughout the day and sometime during the night. There are so many factors that can affect the blood sugar level of a diabetic. My daughter usually awakens at night when her blood sugar levels are low. I had begun to rely on her body to do that.

Nothing prepared me for that night. I woke up suddenly; it was very early in the morning. I felt it was the Holy Spirit. I heard, "Tammy, check on Jadyn." I was so tired and thought my mind was just wandering. A minute later heard I heard the same warning. I tried telling myself that I was just hearing things and that she was okay.

Once again, I heard, "Tammy go check on Jadyn." Reluctantly, I crawled out of bed and walked downstairs. I checked her blood sugar and the meter read low. When this happens it means the levels are too low for the meter to register.

I quickly ran upstairs and grabbed some juice. She refused to drink or cooperate at all. This is a symptom of very low blood sugar. After a few minutes, I finally got her to drink the juice. I had to continue giving her more juice for about another half hour so that the level was high enough to safely let her go back to sleep.

I learned some wonderful lessons about the Holy Spirit that night. Even though we may be tired, or the timing may be inconvenient, the Spirit is there to help us wherever and whenever we might need assistance. I am so grateful God saved my daughter's life that night.

The Spirit Whispered: Please listen to my promptings. I know you are tired but your daughter needs you now! I will give you the strength you need to do what has to be done. Trust in me.

Prayer: Divine Spirit, you are always there to help me when I need you the most. Help me to always be aware and listen to that inner voice that helps me to do what is right.

Tammy Jensen
Energy Healer and Foot Zoner
Lansing, MI

Whisper Forty-Four: Noah, a Birth Story

They say that the second experience of childbirth is always different than the first and often it is shorter. In my case, anything would have been different than the 63 hours of labor, attempted home birth and eventual hospital delivery of our oldest son, Beau.

One Saturday, I took Beau into the city for a day with his cousin, while I savored the tastes of summer with my mom at the local farmer's market. I waddled my pregnant body, munching on green onion cakes, checking out beautiful produce and enjoying the sunshine, while my son was whisked away with his cousin for a bike ride with Grandpa. Then I took my dad with me to Walmart, mainly for his muscles, to buy dog food and had him carry it to my car. We ordered pizza and shared a meal before heading home to meet up with my husband, who had spent the day at the lake with his dad. It had been an eventful day. Little did we know what was going to happen. After a great snuggle and giggle fest with Beau, I put him to bed and went to join Marc in the garage for some chill time.

At 9:20 p.m., I felt the strangest thing as I stood up. It felt and sounded like when you crack your knuckles. Yup, my water broke. We quickly went upstairs and gave our midwife a call. She told me to relax and try to rest, so I did, for all of five minutes. I went back to the bathroom and then into the tub to relax.

Less than an hour later, contractions started. Marc started to track the start time and duration of the contractions, he's so good at that! All I could think about was how exhausted I was and how I hadn't napped. I kept telling Marc random things, where I put this and that, how I was a little afraid, how he couldn't go anywhere...you know, the important stuff!

Contractions picked up quickly, ten minutes apart became four minutes apart. Our midwife arrived and started to set up the birth pool quickly. While I was going through rolling contractions, Marc and our midwife were trying desperately to get as much warm water into the birth pool as they could. I couldn't get into that water fast enough.

Marc got his swimming trunks on and came in with me, not only to help with the water level, but he was catching this baby.

The sensation of birthing a baby, in water, in your house, was perhaps the most amazing thing I had ever experienced. There was a lot of encouragement, while my team of cheerleaders kept me going. I was in a completely different space in my head: praying, focusing and visualizing this new life that we had created. Apparently, I pushed for maybe 20 minutes. Then Marc was placing this little baby onto my chest. He had the cord wrapped loosely around his neck twice (which no one was too concerned about, because it's quite common) and was crying out loud in no time. I DID IT!

I held our baby, with the cord still attached for about 30 minutes in the water, soaking up every ounce of his littleness. Marc cut the cord and we both were still amazed at the experience we had just had. We were smiling. We birthed our baby at home.

While we were walking through the market that morning, my mom had said to me, "Cari, I think you should expect a boy and be surprised by a girl." I knew in my heart that either would be amazingly wonderful. I didn't get my girlie surprise, but I did give birth to an amazing little boy.

Noah Daniel, 7 pounds 5 oz, 20½ inches (or as Marc said "He's 1 foot 8!) at 2:02 a.m. on September 9, 2012.

The Spirit Whispered: You are strong. There isn't a thing you can't do as long as you ask me to be with you. You are built to create life, nurture it and guide it. You are never alone.

Prayer: Divine Spirit, help me to live in the moment, to celebrate, to savor life. You are alive in my life through the lives of our children. You are smiling at me. Enable me to embrace you through the challenges and celebrations in our life.

Cari Letourneau, Early Learning Educator and Mom, Alberta, Canada

Whisper Forty-Five: I Never Give Up!

All my life, I've been told I was a fighter. Being born a premie, my mother swears I've been fighting since the day I was born. It's true what they say, "You never know how strong you are, until being strong is your only option."

To most thirteen-year-olds, strong is being able to do a pull-up in gym class, or simply surviving freshman year in high school. For me, being strong was having surgery to remove my thyroid; which in turn caused weight gain, fluctuations in hormones and emotions, all while trying to survive freshman year.

I then proceeded to tear my ACL while playing volleyball my junior year; additionally I had several "fainting spells" which led to the diagnosis of vasovagal syncope. By the end of my junior year, I had gone to so many doctor appointments that I was ready to just live at the hospital. At one point, I even tried to convince my mom I was suffering from depression, simply because it would explain why life was so difficult for me.

If I had a nickel for every time I asked, "Seriously God, why me?" I could probably pay for my entire college education.

I heard God whisper, "I am here with you and I will never leave you. Trust in me. You will make it through all this a better person."

What I eventually realized is that everyone has their fair share of problems. Mine are no worse than Susie's down the block. And God never gives us anything we can't handle. If my medical experiences have taught me anything, it's that the road blocks and struggles we face are just a part of life. It doesn't matter what challenges come your way. What truly matters is how you react to those challenges and the level of fortitude you develop within yourself to overcome those challenges. After all, it's those challenges that make you who you are.

The Spirit Whispered: I am proud of the woman you are becoming, all those challenges have made you the wonderful loving and caring woman you are. You turned to me when you didn't have any answers. I will always be there for you in your time of need.

Prayer: Divine Spirit, you never gave up on me, you gave me the strength and the grace to continue on when all seemed hopeless. Thanks for loving me so much.

Mallory Martin
Sr. Dorothy's grand niece
Dexter, MI

Whisper Forty-Six: A Call to Compassion

Sometimes we hear God speaking to us through the words of other people. We don't always recognize God's words, but if we listen carefully, we can hear and see God's loving example expressed through the actions of people. I believe God is always there, whether we hear him or not. I believe God is present, even when the news isn't good. However, I don't believe God causes bad things to happen. I have been a District Court Judge for 24 years, and I've seen many types of cases and as a result, a variety of people. Some of those people have shown their very best, and some of those people have shown their very worst. The cases that I oversee can range in seriousness from littering to first degree murder.

One particular case recently really impacted me. It was a very tragic vehicular accident between a school bus and a passenger vehicle. The car was driven by an 86-year-old woman, and her husband was riding with her in the front seat. It was a cold February day, when a 61-year-old school bus driver with 20 years of experience somehow turned in front of the car without seeing it. The collision resulted in the death of the 86-year-old woman driver. Her husband was not seriously injured. The school bus driver could not have felt worse. She was extremely remorseful and will always struggle with how the accident happened. The bus driver was charged criminally with a moving violation causing death. It is punishable by up to one year in jail and $1,000 in fines. It also requires that she lose her driver's license for one year.

Any of us could be in a car accident. We probably all take driving for granted. We never really think we're going to be in a car accident or that anything could happen to us, but it can.

On that February day, lives were changed forever. The loss of this 86-year-old woman was both tragic and heartbreaking. But what I saw and heard in the courtroom renewed my faith in the goodness of humankind.

The bus driver took responsibility for the accident, and pled no contest to the charge of a moving violation causing death. After her plea, I asked the adult son of the 86-year-old victim if he wished to speak. It was as if I could hear God whispering in the courtroom that day as I listened to her son say, "My mother would not want to hold a grudge." He said that his mother always had a desire to go to heaven and that the family honestly believed that it was only God's prerogative to send her there. He truly believed that it was an act of God to send his mother to heaven. As far as the bus driver, he said, "I feel sorry for her, and I want to support her and plead for leniency on her behalf." It was an amazing thing to hear, such compassion, such empathy. The family of the 86-year-old woman had forgiven the bus driver. I knew in an instant that love, compassion, and understanding would allow both of these families to heal.

God teaches us that compassion is an important virtue. Compassion is a necessary part of the healing process. The fact that the family of this 86-year-old woman could forgive the bus driver, and actually ask for leniency for her was like watching God's love in action.

The bus driver was suffering in a different way than the family of the 86-year-old woman who died, but her suffering was real. Hearing the family's genuine words of forgiveness was healing for all of us, but certainly it allowed the bus driver to begin to forgive herself.

When it came time for the bus driver to speak, she looked right at the family of the dear 86-year-old woman, and expressed her sincere and heartfelt sympathy to them. She spoke openly in court and with great emotion. She also thanked all her family members, friends, and co-workers who had supported her throughout this extremely difficult experience.

It was interesting, that of the several letters I received from people connected to both the bus driver and the victim, both of these women were described as truly special human beings. The words used to describe both of them were almost interchangeable: kind, loving, heart of gold, always willing to help others. I knew both of these women were exceptional people.

While I realized I had to impose a sentence, I knew that compassion was what was really needed. There would be no jail sentence, only words of encouragement and forgiveness. A standard fine was assessed and a request to do community service, something that would benefit others.

It was an amazing experience to see the two families embrace at the end of the Court's sentencing. It was both heartwarming and refreshing to see God's love displayed between families that were once strangers and now shared a bond that is simply indescribable. As a judge, I am accustomed to dealing with victims of crime that are so full of hatred and anger that forgiveness seems to be the farthest thing from their mind. But the family members of this beautiful, loving, kind and compassionate 86-year-old woman were able to pay tribute to their loved one by forgiving the bus driver. By listening to God, they chose compassion.

It was an exceptionally emotional experience in the courtroom. After the court proceeding, my clerk mentioned to me that she felt as if she had just been at a church service. I think that day in court we all heard the divine whisper of the one who teaches compassion, love, understanding, and forgiveness.

We can all take a lesson from the family of this 86-year-old woman who was killed. Her husband and her sons had truly heard Jesus telling them, "She is in heaven." They found peace and forgiveness by expressing compassion for the school bus driver. Through that compassion, they listened to their hearts. They are now able to be at peace and experience the healing touch of God. Perhaps even more important, through their compassion they were able to forgive the bus driver who is on the road to healing herself.

The Spirit Whispered: Do not hold a grudge. You are a witness of God's love when you forgive. Your compassion will help you heal.

Prayer: Divine Spirit, thank you for giving people who are hurting the ability to be compassionate. Thank you for teaching us that compassion and kindness can enable us to heal from heartache and pain. Thank you for allowing us to forgive, so that we too may be healed.

Sara J. Smolenski
Chief Judge of the 63rd District Court
Grand Rapids, MI

Whisper Forty-Seven: A Miracle for 30 Weeks Please

It doesn't matter how much time has passed since my story took place, I believe when you listen to your inner voice, it will lead you where you are meant to be. Each time I've tried to ignore that voice, or "hush" it, I never felt at peace. It only took about 30 years, but I've learned and I didn't learn in a small way.

I was almost six months into my second pregnancy when I became aware of the cautionary whispers. They began like feathery branches brushing against my shoulder, only gaining my attention when I sat silent and mindful in the moment. My first daughter was a tender nine months old and I was giddy with happiness, my world full of new and amazing moments at each turn. As with many new mothers, I wanted to be all and do all. I was organized, hard-working and expected the most from myself and everyone around me. I was determined to have it all and downright demanded it from myself.

I also knew something was heading my way and there would be no hiding from it. Something was going wrong with the baby inside me. The more I ignored it, the louder and stronger the whispers became. At 23 weeks, I knew the baby would barely be viable. The statistics were there in black and white. The likelihood of her living through a premature birth was only around 17%. At 30 weeks, the percentage went up to 90%! I had to make it to 30 weeks and I needed to get the doctors to take a closer look at her. I mentioned my feelings to my husband and we prayed together. We prayed a lot and we prayed big! I had some private conversations with God, too. There was shameless bartering on my part. Promises were made and begging ensued, "Please protect her and let me get to 30 weeks!" I told the doctors about the feeling I was having. They told me not to worry and everything looked great. I was healthy, the baby was developing on schedule and all was good, except, it wasn't. At 26 weeks, I started bleeding a little. Still, the doctors insisted all was normal. No prescribed bed rest suggested. No ultrasound ordered. Heartbeat's fine. Baby's fine. Mommy's fine. All is well. My inner voice yelled, "No it's not!"

I could count on one hand, the times I have told an outright lie during my lifetime. The first time I told a lie was to my dad, at age 10. I lied to save my sister's backside. As a teenager, she had snuck out of the house. When he came looking for her, I told my dad she was upstairs sleeping. He believed me. Now I had another person to save. Her name was Meghan. She was in danger. What started as whispers were now alarm bells driving me to constant distraction and shifting my focus, constantly back and forth between alternatives and outcomes. I thought I might go mad! It was time. I called the doctor and lied. I made up a story about how my 11 month old daughter had accidently kicked me in the belly really hard. It got me on the schedule to be examined the following week.

At this point, I began to release my "perceived" grip and stopped trying to control everything. I am not sure if it was a conscious choice or if I had simply surrendered from exhaustion. My center had shifted. It was no longer about the fact that something was wrong, but rather, how am I going to get through this? I started to listen more closely to that inner voice and make decisions as each moment commanded them. I showed up at the doctor's on a Monday afternoon even though my appointment was for Tuesday. They saw me anyway because it was a 30-minute drive from my home. They took blood and told me if they found anything wrong, they would call right away and have me come back in for further examination. Tuesday went by without incident. Wednesday, I felt some mild relief as they hadn't called and went on about my day. At approximately 11 a.m. the hospital called my office and asked that I come in to be monitored and scheduled for an ultrasound. "It was nothing to be alarmed about, just precautionary," they said. I left work and went home.

I called my mother and my sister and told them the story. Both calls were out of the ordinary. Neither of them knew anything had been wrong, but I had been nudged. I told the nanny not to wake my husband who had worked all night, as he would likely need the sleep in the days to come. After another nudge, I packed up my bag, got in the car, stopped at the bank, the spa, and the post office, checking things off my eternal to-do list. Nudge. Nudge. Nudge. I arrived at the hospital at 1:00 p.m. I was placed on the monitor by 1:30 p.m. My doctor was at the hospital on his lunch hour checking on another patient. He stopped by to say hello, and as he left, his words were, "We will have you home in time for dinner!" I sat and waited to be seen in radiology.

At two o'clock, after a sudden sharp pain, I started to hemorrhage. It was so severe my blood pressure had bottomed out sounding an alarm in the nurses' station. My pulse was almost non-existent. I was dying and so was the baby. I was alone, scared and wide-eyed...but only for a moment. As I was rushed to the OR in that tiny small town hospital with doctors and nurses yelling and scrambling around me, I knew everything had led to this moment. Each person present at that time was nothing short of divine intervention. The head nurse, who was the only trained staff member in neonatology, was only on site that day because she had scheduled a meeting with the local pediatrician. The pediatrician was literally walking in the door to the hospital for that meeting when his emergency pager went off. The anesthesiologist happened to be administering an epidural for another expectant mother down the hall, and my doctor hadn't quite left the hospital to go back to his office when his emergency pager went off. Had one person been out of step, I wouldn't be here writing this story, nor would I be looking at my second daughter sitting only a few feet from me. Born at 2:18 p.m., 30 weeks along, Meghan entered this world suffocated from blood and so ill that many thought she would not survive a week. If she did, her quality of life would likely be poor.

Years later, as I watch her put her book aside to stretch her willowy arms and legs before jumping up to chase the family cat, I marvel at her long hair piled up in a loose bun, her beautiful eyes burning with mischief and the smile she sends my way before running off. Oh! How grateful I am and inspired over and over again! For not only does she lead a fulfilling life, she deeply enriches the lives of those around her.

The Spirit Whispered: Listen to me, do what you know will be right for you and your child.

Prayer: Divine Spirit, help me listen to your messages. Help me to reflect upon your work in my life so that I may better serve you and those around me.

Tracey Mullaney
CPA
East Lansing, MI

Whisper Forty-Eight: You Are Just Where I Want You To Be

Four years ago, I was starting a new job in a new area of the company. My desk was temporarily located within our call center team. I was seated between two fiery red heads. One was about my age and very professional, and the other was younger and definitely a little rough around the edges. During the first week of work, I kept hearing different people talk about how God puts you where you need to be, when you need to be there and with the people whom you need. In fact, I heard this theme so many times, that I knew God was trying to tell me something.

At the end of the first week, I noticed that the younger red head was really trying hard to make a connection with me. My first reaction was to distance myself from her. That's when the little voice in my head said, "Don't turn your back on her," and I started thinking about all of the stories I heard about being exactly where you are needed and with the people who need you. Remembering this caused me to see things in a different light and I gave this woman a chance. Instead of thinking how strangely this young woman was acting, I saw her actions as a cry for attention and a need for acceptance.

I opened myself to really listen and learn what made her who she was and why our paths were crossing. The more I learned about her, the more impressed I was with this true survivor whom God had placed in my life. This beautiful, fiery, feisty woman's life had been very difficult and unpleasant. Despite everything, she had stayed true to herself and her desire to make a good life for herself. She had a horribly abusive mother who had hurt her with verbal and physical violence. She had been in and out of multiple foster homes where the foster families treated her like an unwanted outcast, and she had lived part of the time with a grandmother who didn't know how to help her. She also didn't have a father growing up. Her mother refused to tell her who her father was, and the men that came and went from their house either didn't pay her any attention or gave her the wrong kind of attention.

She had her first child, a son, at the age of 15. She tried to raise him while going to high school, but after two months, realized she couldn't do it on her own. She feared that she was becoming abusive toward her son, so she contacted her case worker and asked for help. The case worker contacted the father's family and they agreed to take custody of the child. As hard as it was to give up her child, she did so out of love. She graduated from high school with the help of a wonderful school counselor and mentor. This counselor was the first person in her life who believed in her and encouraged her to make a better life for herself.

After graduating she met and quickly married her first husband, who was an abusive man. Her stories about their married life were grim with the exception of the times they had his children with them. She loved those kids and really enjoyed spending time with them. After two years, she gave birth to her daughter. It was around this time that she found her own father.

Her mother had only told her bits and pieces about her father. This smart, savvy woman put all the pieces together to figure out who her father was. She took a huge risk and called him. She asked him if he had dated her mother and he said yes. When she told him she thought he was her father, he asked to meet her. This started the first positive relationships in her life, not only with her father but her stepmother and her half-siblings as well.

After her daughter was born, her husband treated her better than he had in the past, so she stayed and tried to be a good wife and mother. After about two years, she got scared that she was turning into her mother again, so she asked for a divorce, gave her daughter to her ex-husband, and joined the Navy.

She thrived in the Navy for about a year. Then, due to some serious medical issues that left her unable to serve any longer, she was honorably discharged. Her service had earned her a naval scholarship which allowed her to start going to college. Over the next two years, she married a second abusive man, but still kept moving forward with her education, determined to achieve her dream of creating a good life for herself. Eventually, she decided she needed out of the second marriage and moved closer to home. That is how she ended up working at the same company with me.

As I learned about her, I came to appreciate who she was and understood why she was missing some essential skills needed to be successful in the work place. I started mentoring her. Because she had such a strong fight or flight instinct, she wanted to quit and just walk away from her job any time she had a bad day. Slowly, she started making progress in building her professionalism.

Through all of this, we built a strong friendship. I was able to watch her grow, as well as assist her through setbacks. She continued to excel in her classes and was finally one semester away from earning her bachelor's degree. She started researching what it would take to go to law school and pass her LSATs. Then, a month before graduation, tragedy struck.

She was driving back to her dad's house located out in the country. No one knows exactly what caused this to happen, but her car swerved over the center line and hit an oncoming car. The other driver was killed instantly, but, true to herself to the end, she fought to hang onto life. She lived for about six hours before passing away.

Her short life ended, but the lessons she taught me will stay with me for the rest of my life.

The Spirit Whispered: Don't judge others by your first impression. Listen and learn each person's story. Try to truly understand them and be open to what you can learn from them. I will help you be God's presence to others.

Prayer: Divine Spirit, open our hearts to see others as you see them. Let us learn to love first and accept those you bring into our lives.

Deborah E.W. Heiss
Analyst
Battle Creek, MI

*"May the God of Hope
Fill you with all Joy and Peace
as you Trust in Him,
so that you may overflow with Hope
by the Power of the Holy Spirit."*

Romans 15:13

Whisper Forty-Nine: He Shouts

It was a shout, "Don't worry about it, I'll take care of it!" I was used to his whispers. That inner voice that you know is God speaking to you. But this time, it came as a shout. It was May 1984, and I was reviewing the state of my life and my frustration that there was no one "out there" to spend the rest of my life with. I had met plenty of women, but none of them seemed to be the right one. But when God shouts, it's a good idea to listen. So I put aside my efforts and left it up to him to figure it out.

The summer of 1984 was a busy one between work and graduate studies. That autumn brought a heightened busyness, but there was still an empty dance card. Autumn also meant University of Michigan football. My three college buddies and I had bought pairs of season football tickets, optimistically, thinking that someday someone would want to share the excitement of Michigan football with us. Three of the four guys had reached their dream with their life-mate firmly planted in the bleacher seat next to them; however, the seat next to me was empty. That was, until a surprise guest, Kristin, joined us at the invitation of one of the couples. We naturally sat next to each other (the other seats were taken!) and we had a great time talking, nearly missing most of the game.

After the game, we all spent time at a tailgate party and then decided to go out to a movie on campus. Kristin was not able to join us because she had lesson plans to do in preparation for her up-coming work week as a teacher. Although disappointed, I moved on making a note that this surprise guest seemed very nice. There was one potentially large obstacle to overcome if we were to have a relationship. She was a devout Catholic and I was a committed Protestant.

I was anticipating some type of shout from God confirming that this was the woman he had for me. However the only shouting I heard was at the football game where we were cheering our team to victory. Otherwise...silence.

That silence remained until the end of the football season when I was hosting a meeting with a group of prominent local business-men; a shout came in the form of an emergency phone call. The secretary came into the conference room announcing, "Mr. Dolsen, you have an urgent phone call." I left the conference room and went to the phone. I was nervous about what this emergency could be. It was my roommate, Fernando, who had invited Kristin to the football game. "Dan, this is Fernando. If you have ever thought about asking Kristin Lundberg out, you must do it this weekend"—Click.

That was it? This was urgent? I returned to my meeting. Later that day I did respond to the emergency and called Kristin to ask her out.

By the time we did go out, an entire football season had passed since we had first met. I had been busy dating other young women, seeking the woman God had for me, so this felt like just another date. And although this date was inspired by a shout over the phone, the shout was muted by me because of the difference in religion. So this second encounter came with some real doubts as to whether or not this was the "one."

After picking up Kristin to drive to a Sunday brunch in downtown Ann Arbor, we made our way to our table enjoying the pleasantries of small talk. How was church? Is work going well? Did you watch the game yesterday?

And as we were taking our seats, there was a shout! It was the same shout I had heard in May. That clear inner voice of God saying, "This is the one, don't get all excited or weird—just go forward with confidence." Although I was confused over God's choice of the word "weird," it was clearly a shout! Many months later I told Kristin about this experience. What she vividly remem-bered was that we both were sitting down, we glanced at each other and she had a strong sense that this was going to be a sig-nificant time, like no other date. So whether it was a shout, or a "strong sense," it explains what happened next....

As we sat together and brunch was served, I looked at Kristin and with a certain degree of seriousness said, "I'm going to lay the cards on the table. I know you're Catholic and I'm Protestant so let's get the big question out of the way, are you open to dating a Protestant?" Kristin quickly responded, "I'm open to whatever God wants for me and would enjoy getting to know you better."

We did enjoy getting to know each other better. We learned great lessons about appreciating each other's gifts and differences, including the gift of the differences we held in our two denominations.

But our differences went a lot deeper than simple denominational differences. What we discovered was that the two of us approached our faith from two different perspectives. Kristin's faith starts with her heart. She has a deep love for Jesus that is often expressed through the love and compassion she shows others. My faith starts in my head and eventually gets to my heart. Simply, I need some degree of intellectual understanding before I move to a point of heartfelt faith.

For some couples, these different approaches can create a point of conflict, much as denominational differences can bring about conflict. But with a heavy dose of God's grace and the deep respect that we hold for one another, we have embraced these differences. We see them as contributing to the richness of our relationship both as a married couple and with God. We choose not to try to change each other, but instead, to take on each other's differences. I try to bring more of my heart to my faith. Kristin has focused more intently on gaining an intellectual appreciation for Christianity.

The same is true of our denominational differences. We do this by first acknowledging our unity in Jesus and the unity God has established in us as husband and wife. We then seek out opportunities to support each other in the essentials of our faith. For Kristin, it is expressed through participating in a local Rosary group. For me, it means her joining me for a Sunday worship service. For both of us, it means spending time together in daily prayer, the study of scripture and reaching out to others.

So what started as a shout from God, led to a "call." A call to be one. To be united. And to remember, he really does know what he is doing. So listen, because sometimes, he does shout!

The Spirit Whispered: Don't worry about it! I'll take care of it!

Prayer: Divine Spirit, help me to listen to you and to trust you in every part of my life.

Dan Dolsen [wife Kristin]
Commercial Real Estate Executive
Saline, MI

Whisper Fifty: Why Am I Doing This?

I grew up in Moscow, Russia. A couple of months every summer, my family would go to our cottage in the countryside. We would pick wild mushrooms, herbs, and berries in the nearby forest with my grandmother and she would spend time explaining their medicinal properties. My grandmother showed me how to extract and prepare them for winter.

My mom was a patent attorney specializing in chemistry inventions. My dad had a degree in Engineering Physics. I grew up in a very scientific family with a completely holistic lifestyle. My parents would not buy clothes made from synthetic fibers or food with artificial color or flavor additives. They did not believe those substances were beneficial for our health. Sometimes my sister and I would complain about it, but my mom would always say, "I'm doing this because I really understand chemistry, and that's why you're not getting it." Today I am grateful to my parents for their progressive views. Looking back it's easy to understand why I chose to become a cosmetic formulator with a completely holistic philosophy.

In 1991, my husband was offered a job in Texas and my newborn son and I moved with him. It was our first trip to America. In addition to being a mom during my first three years in America, I worked on my English, transferred my credentials from Russia, and became a licensed esthetician. Soon after, my husband got another job offer to teach at the University of Southern Mississippi, and I found myself formulating products for a plastic surgeon's office and working at a spa in the heart of the Deep South. It was very difficult to find natural and organic ingredients, and many people couldn't understand why I wanted to use such an "old-fashioned" approach. I had to import the dried plants and oils from abroad. It took me several years to develop my first small, five product skin-care line, but I was very proud of the fact that they were corrective, natural and even edible!

In 1998, in the middle of a hot, sticky summer, we left Mississippi and moved to Michigan. My husband was offered a position at Western Michigan University as a professor teaching viola. Our son was about to enter second grade. It was such a relief to leave the muggy heat of the South. For seven long years, I had missed the beauty and magic of nature in the north.

I came to Michigan with a true desire to implement my vision and philosophy 100%. To be able to do this without compromising, I had to start my own business. On September 1, 1998, I opened Elina Herbal Skin Care Clinic in Kalamazoo, Michigan. As a small business owner, I knew that opening the door doesn't come with a guarantee that a lot of customers will walk through it. It takes time to develop clientele and create a good reputation. I was a well-known professional when we lived in the south, and my schedule was very busy. I wasn't used to being alone in my treatment room. Little by little, the clients started coming to my new clinic. I really wanted to make sure that I could give them the results they wanted, so I was formulating and adjusting my serums and lotions for each person.

When I had extra time in my schedule, I would turn a 90-minute facial into a 3 hour appointment without charging extra. I also worked with some clients who were going through challenging financial times. Some of them were students with cystic acne who needed lots of attention, deep detoxifying and healing skin treatments a few times a month. Some were women whose husbands had lost their jobs. There were two hard-working single moms, one nurse and one teacher, who couldn't afford the skin treatments and products needed for their problem complexions. There were many others who couldn't afford my services, but I provided them anyway.

The combined cost of my unique natural ingredients, lease, and bills were quite high and it started to worry me. I felt guilty for leaving my young son with a babysitter for hours to work for free. One day I exited my office and stood in the parking lot. I looked up at the grey sky and asked the Spirit, "Why am I doing this?" I continued to give so much of myself day after day. There was a very clear answer that came to my mind and heart. The answer was, "You are doing this because that's what you're supposed to do. Just keep taking care of people in a loving way and don't worry. Keep doing what you're doing." After hearing and truly feeling that voice in me, I felt like a weight was lifted from my entire body. It reinforced my beliefs. In just a few months after that experience, my business grew significantly. While I was now completely booked with paying clients, I never stopped helping those in need.

Today I own spas in Kalamazoo, Michigan and Chicago, Illinois. Elina Organics has been named "Chicago's Best Facial" by Chicago Magazine. My products are sold in salons and doctors' offices across the country. I am very fortunate to work with wonderful and spiritual professionals, who bring a loving, caring approach to our clients.

Seven years ago I started the Association of Holistic Skin-Care Practitioners. We provide education to skin care professionals who are trying to work beyond the surface and consider health on many levels, including body, mind, and spirit. The association: helps us find each other, provides mutual support, and spreads our message to more professionals. All of the members of our group are deeply spiritual people. Every day we start with prayer or meditation to connect to the highest source. It helps us to get guidance and stay on the right path. The Divine Spirit's guidance helps us make it through the challenging times with peace and trust in our hearts.

The Spirit Whispered: You are doing this because that's what you're supposed to do. Just keep taking care of people in a loving way and don't worry. Keep doing what you're doing.

Prayer: Divine Spirit, please continue to give me clarity and guidance in all that I do. May angels surround and support me through every step of my journey.

Elina Fedotova
Owner of Elina Organic Cosmetics
Kalamazoo, MI

---❖---

*"I knew nothing but love and devotion
when I was growing up.
Trust me, it makes
everything easier."*

Julia Quinn

---❖---

186

Whisper Fifty-One: The Spirit Works through Grams and Gramps

I am the oldest of four children. I was my paternal grandparents' first grandchild. I was the apple of their eye. I loved them beyond words. My grandfather, who was actually my father's stepfather, was my Godfather, and he also named me. Until I was eight years old, my grandparents, Grams and Gramps as I called them, lived two blocks from my family in the suburbs of Detroit.

That summer, Gramps semi-retired, and they bought a small motel in Christmas, Michigan. Both my grandparents were born and raised in the Upper Peninsula. This move was their opportunity to return home to spend time with their siblings and extended family, while fulfilling their goal of being motel owners. Their move rocked my eight-year-old world; a world where I shared weekends and holidays with Grams and Gramps, which included Sunday Mass and a trip to the grocery store after Mass to purchase ice cream and any flavor of Faygo pop my heart desired.

I spent most of my summer vacations with my grandparents at the motel. I cherished my time with them, and learned many life lessons through watching and helping. I learned how to treat people/ customers, how to run a business, about the many wonderful places to visit in the U.P., about my grandparents' family and about my grandparents—their faith, compassion, and commitment. I watched my grandfather put a bottle of champagne in a newlywed couple's motel room when they'd left to see the sites, and the countless number of times Gramps was rousted from his sleep at all hours of the night to accommodate a late night traveler or offer a stranded motorist the phone in the middle of the night. He provided directions and recommendations, and the tiny 12-unit motel would have return reservations year after year. He was a loving soul, with a devout faith that he lived by example every day of his life.

Each winter, my grandparents would leave the U.P. and spend winters in the Detroit area near our family. Eventually, I hit my teen years; my family left the Detroit area for northern Lower Michigan.

My grandparents determined that Michigan winters were not warm enough and they began to winter in Florida. Due in part to my familiarity with the U.P., my love of "God's Country," and knowing that my grandparents were a mere 45 miles away, I elected to attend Northern Michigan University. My parents were apprehensive about my being so far from home. On the other hand, my grandparents were elated. As much as my course load would allow, I would spend weekends with my grandparents. Grams would fill me up with home cooking, and we would travel to different areas of the U.P. on Sundays after Mass.

My senior year of college, Gramps passed away in his sleep two days before Christmas. Our family was devastated. Grams ran the motel for the next five years by herself. I would help out on weekends. I worried about her being there by herself, but she carried on. Grams and I became even closer. We talked often and discussed everything. On one of my visits I found a penny, and Grams shared that when we find pennies, they are reminders that our angels are with us and watching over us.

Grams shared many prayers with me over the years for all occasions, i.e. the prayer to St. Anthony for lost articles, "Tony, Tony, please come down, something's lost that must be found" and when whatever was lost was found, and it always was, you said a prayer to St. Anthony in thanks.

If you are blessed to live long enough, you lose loved ones. We lost Grams at the age of 76. I witnessed the Holy Spirit in the love I shared with my grandparents, and the love they shared with so many people. They were wonderful examples of God's love.

About 10 years after Grams had passed, my younger sister Angela, a 36-year-old, married LPN, mother of four young children was diagnosed with breast cancer. Our family and friends supported Angie throughout her ten-year battle; I asked Angie if Grams had shared the story about pennies. My sister had no clue, so I shared what Grams had told me: that angels watch over us, that they were with us and reminded us by leaving us pennies. So each time I would pray for my sister Angie and would find pennies I would give them to Angie. We would call each other when we found pennies. We knew that Grams was "watching over us" and heard our prayers.

My sister has resided in heaven for the past three years. Since she made her journey I have prayed for guidance and strength especially as I was finishing my last semester of college in 2013. I continue to find pennies when my mind is heavy with worry or doubt. I have faith that everything will be just fine because my angels are watching over me.

The Spirit Whispered: Come to me when your mind and heart are heavy. Do not give up, trust me. I will always watch over you.

Prayer: Divine Spirit, may I be a witness of your love like my grandparents were to everyone they met. Be with me and guide me every day of my life.

Heidi K. Brown
Vice President Administration
Lansing, MI

―――――・◆・―――――

"She smiled at and spoke
to each person.
It was as though she couldn't
come into contact
with anyone or anything
without imparting some of her
goodness
onto them."

M. Leighton

―――――・◆・―――――

Whisper Fifty-Two: Two Bible Verses That Changed My Life

I thought I had to be in control of my life, if I wasn't who would be? I was a single mom and my son was in high school when I had my awakening! I was working hard in my career, raising an active son, and keeping a household running. There were voids in my life and I was filling them through empty relationships and shopping. One can only imagine how life was. Stress, rushing—a surface level life.

I was in a breakfast meeting one morning, and I was talking with a woman who I knew through business. I had shared a little about my life's struggles, and she shared Jeremiah 29:11 with me. She said, "Shari, God has a plan for you and it will be a good plan." I believed in God, but knew very little about the bible. This intrigued me so I went home, dug out my bible, and looked for this verse. Amazing! To think God had plans for me! I knew nothing of talking decisions over with God, letting him direct my steps, or a real relationship with Jesus Christ. This opened my eyes to bigger things. I decided I wanted to know more. Growing up Catholic and attending Catholic junior and senior high, I felt the need to get back to my roots.

I attended a 6:30 Wednesday morning Mass. I heard Fr. Klein read and talk about Galatians 5:22. Wow! Fruits of the Spirit! I thought, "This is how I want to live." I need to know more about this and how to apply it to my life. I went off to work, but that night on the way home I stopped at Barnes and Noble. When I need to know more about something, my answer has always been to find a book. I was perusing the Christian section of the bookstore. A book jumped out at me, *A Woman's Walk with God*. I really felt led to this particular book, and the title sounded like the answer. Once home with the book, I looked closer and the subtitle of this book was, *Growing in the Fruits of the Spirit*, a whole book about living a life through the Fruits of the Spirit. It was precisely what my goal was that morning! God led me to the exact book I needed! This book by Elizabeth George changed my life! I learned how Jesus was asking me to live, what each Fruit of the Spirit means here in this life and how to apply them to every day. I felt my heart and actions changing.

I continued my study on the Fruits of the Spirit throughout the year and beyond. At this same time, I continued to pray on Jeremiah 29:11, "For surely I know the plans I have for you, says the Lord, plans for your welfare and not for harm, to give you a future with hope."

The Holy Spirit was a big part of my life now, and my prayer life was strong. I prayed about Jeremiah 29:11 for two years as to where God wanted me. My son was now in college, and I spent a lot of time reading and studying my bible. I asked God if marriage could be a part of my life. If so, I prayed that he send me a man he wanted in my life, a man who would share my faith and was part of his plan for me. This is what was missing in my empty relationships and past marriage, God. This was very important to me. I would not settle for less. As I studied the Fruits and continued to learn what it means to be a Godly woman, mother, and hopefully a wife again, I felt that God was preparing me for something.

By this time, I was feeling peace and joy deep within me through Jesus and the Holy Spirit. Two years after I started to pray Jeremiah 29:11 and truly watch and listen for God's plan, I met Duane. On our first date, we talked for three hours straight. We had similar life journeys, he had just been confirmed Catholic about three weeks prior, and we experienced an immediate connection. About two weeks after we started dating, Duane invited me to his home for dinner. Our relationship was already growing as we had deep talks each day. As I walked into his home the very first thing I saw hanging on the wall was a plaque with the bible verse from Jeremiah 29:11. I stopped and asked God, "Is this the plan?" I felt God speak to me; he was showing me this is the plan. He directed my steps to Duane. Six months later Duane and I were married.

When I look back over the past 12 years, these two bible versus have blessed my life beyond measure. I lean on them to this day and use them as a foundation for living.

With God's blessing, Duane and I are entering our tenth year of marriage; my son is grown and married with a baby of his own. Through my marriage to Duane, I have two beautiful step-daughters who are grown with families of their own. We are a blended, God-loving family.

I still pull out my Fruits of the Spirit book to keep me on track and I also pray and quote Jeremiah 29:11 often. Of course through the years I have built a library of favorite bible verses that guide my life. My relationship with Jesus Christ continues to grow, and I know my foundation sits with my two favorite verses; Galatians 5:22 and Jeremiah 29:11.

The Spirit Whispered: I have plans for your life. Trust in me. Through the Fruits of the Holy Spirit, I was asking you to be patient and wait for my timing. I want you to continue to live as a woman who follows God using the Fruits as your guide.

Prayer: Divine Spirit, please continue to direct my steps and help me to always choose the most loving choice each day by living as a Godly woman. It is easy to get busy and distracted. Thank you for keeping me close. Through your grace and mercy may I be a blessing each day to my husband, family, and friends.

Shari Pash Berger, Owner
Strategic Solutions for Growth, Consultant, Trainer
Lansing, MI

———— • ————

"In the garden I tend to drop my
thoughts here and there.
To the flowers I whisper the
secrets I keep
and the hopes I breathe.
I know they are there
to eavestdrop for the angels."

Dodinsky

———— • ————

Whisper Fifty-Three: Amazing Grace

My husband and I were married just a few months when we decided to start a family. We both always knew we wanted to have many children. After four to five months of trying to conceive without any success, I started to panic. Fear and worry began to consume me.

I was raised *with* a strong faith and always felt like I *had* a strong faith, but suddenly realized I had never been tested with something so difficult. I began praying constantly but just could not get over the strong feelings of hopelessness and lack of control. I had some days that were harder than others. On the very worst of days, I heard the song "Amazing Grace." Sometimes, it was at Mass, but other times were random. I came out of work one afternoon and heard bells nearby playing the hymn. Another time, I was lying on the couch in a depressed mess and came across someone singing it on a PBS special. The Spirit whispered to me through this song. I realized that God was with me through all of this and I had to trust his plan.

Two years to the month that we started trying, I became pregnant and in August of 2001, I had my sweet baby boy. I was sure I would have a girl and we'd name her "Grace" but I was so blessed with an amazing son! To complete the story we took Griffin to his very first Mass, and to my surprise "Amazing Grace," naturally, was the recessional song.

The Spirit Whispered: I am with you during this time of doubt and fear. Trust me and all things will be provided to you.

Prayer: Divine Spirit, I know you are near. Help me to trust and believe that you will help me get through this time of fear and worry and remember these words:

"Amazing grace! How sweet the sound,
That saved a wretch like me.
I once was lost, but now am found,
Was blind, but now I see.

Was grace that taught my heart to fear,
And grace my fears relieved.
How precious did that grace appear,
The hour I first believed."

Mary Chris Hotchkiss, Sales Manager
Greater Lansing Convention and Visitors Bureau
East Lansing, MI

Whisper Fifty-Four: Julie, Cancer, Butterflies and Hospice

My husband, Mike, and I met Julie and Kevin in Lamaze class 25 years ago. We hit it off with them from the instant we met—and almost got kicked out of the birth preparation class because we had way too much fun! Our oldest children were born a few days apart and our paths crossed often over the next several years.

We lived in the same town, attended the same church and watched our children grow up. We bonded in several ways, our faith in common. Julie was an inspiration to many, her light and faith always shining.

In 2004, Julie experienced a severe headache and difficulty speaking. She went to the ER and was immediately admitted to the hospital. Julie had a malignant brain tumor. She did not let this define her; she fought through her treatment, many surgeries and complications for the next few years.

In the summer of 2007, Kevin called me and asked for my help. He needed someone to help with her care while he was at work. The financial stress was very difficult. At this time, their two girls were in high school. When Kevin called me, I immediately said, "Yes, I will be there tomorrow." I will never forget driving up the hill to their house. I said, "Lord please help me, I do not know why I said I could do this because I don't know what I'm doing!" The Spirit whispered, "It will be okay." Over the next several months, I was faced with many things I had not experienced in my life. At first, Julie could communicate and eat, but slowly she had to accept assistance with everything. She shared with me that she was ready for heaven, but leaving her girls was very difficult. Of course, this was very stressful for her family.

Her light and faith still shone through and the Lord helped me face her death. I was doing things I didn't know I was capable of, being a caretaker.

Eventually, Julie accepted hospice care and her journey to heaven was near. On the day Julie passed, I was at a yoga class in the morning. I practiced in a closed room with the instructor. I was anticipating a call from Kevin at any moment. During that hour, a butterfly came into the room. It probably came from under the door, I'm not sure, but I was very surprised. The butterfly circled my head and left. When I got outside to my car, the butterfly was on my rearview mirror! On the way home, I received a call from Kevin, telling me to come and say goodbye to my friend. The Lord whispered to me, through the butterfly. To this day, I am reminded of Julie when I see a butterfly.

I had thought many times during my days with Julie, how honored and thankful I was to be at her side. I was inspired and committed to helping others. So, a few months after Julie passed, I trained to be a hospice volunteer. I volunteered to be a patient companion. I was privileged to meet many people facing illness and death. I learned so much.

In 2009, my best friend, Kristin,was diagnosed with colon cancer. God had prepared me for this challenging time. I was able to be strong and to support her through her treatment and healing. He also showed me a talent that I did not know I had, how to be a caretaker. One of Kristin's favorite verses is Romans 8:28, "And we know that in all things God works for the good of those who love him, who have been called according to his purpose." God whispered to me through this verse also. The Spirit whispered to me through these experiences and showed me how God can work through me. I now work for hospice and hope to touch people daily.

The Spirit Whispered: I know your heart and what you can do, let me work through you to help others.

Prayer: Divine Spirit, I thank you each day as you lead me to do this work. It continues to bring me closer to you, a reward beyond all rewards.

Amy Cattell
Annual Giving Coordinator, Arbor Hospice
Saline, MI

Whisper Fifty-Five: Flurries and Fog

Michigan: land of government bailouts and factory closures, frigidly cold temperatures and gray skies, nasally accents and mid western colloquialisms like "pop" instead of soda.

We had just celebrated our fifth anniversary. We had settled into our first home, and were enjoying the beauty and warmth of Carolina blue skies when my husband departed for a second job interview in Michigan. And he seemed excited.

I passively prayed for God's will to unfold through the interview process. *I knew* God's will was for us to stay in the comfort of our current home, in the jobs we currently enjoyed, surrounded by family and the friendships we had built over the previous 13 years. So I kissed my husband goodbye, as I dropped him off at the airport, and wished him well on the grueling 24 hour interview process he had before him. Somewhat smugly I drove away, back to what was comfortable and known, prepared to pick him up the next day and wait patiently for the day when I would offer him love and support after he heard that the potential employer had decided to go in a different direction. We would then go back to planning for the expansion of our back deck and decide where our son would attend preschool the following fall. Michigan would become a distant memory.

That evening Paul called after his grueling interview and he sounded energized and excited. He told me about all the people he met, the great work that was happening and what he would be doing should he be hired. Quite frankly I hadn't heard him that excited about anything in quite a long time, certainly not work-related. And that excitement continued when just days later he received a call that he was a finalist and they wanted to fly both of us to Michigan for a final interview. So we left the mild temperatures, blue skies and headed for the flurries and fog of February in Michigan. I spent the day touring our potential new home, eating at lovely places and politely participating in conversations all the while knowing we were **not** going to end up here.

We were not! We were not? We were.

As we dined on Italian delicacies for our final meal in Ann Arbor, an envelope was slipped across the table to Paul, which included in writing the offer they were making for him to join their staff. As we went back to the hotel to discuss our options, I felt a flutter within and the Spirit whispered, "It is time. Trust in me."

Together we sat and weighed the pros and cons: all that we would be leaving, but all the adventures that could be gained. I would be leaving a job that I loved, but Paul had an opportunity for a sizable promotion. While we recognized all we would be saying goodbye to, the answer became clear through the night that our decision was indeed to move to Michigan.

I geared up for the necessary transitions nearly as soon as we hit ground back in North Carolina, where it was 75° and sunny, as the move was to happen in two months. First we would tearfully tell our immediate family and then our co-workers who had become like family. We met with a realtor, began to paint over our colorful walls in various hues of beige and finally got to those overgrown bushes to improve our curb appeal. Each night I began to pack a box or two. First, I removed all the personalized items from the walls and shelves, wrapped those most precious and delicate belongings in layers of bubble wrap to be unpacked in another place some time yet to come. So, too, I personally felt the stripping away and letting go as we prepared for our moving date. The bare walls mimicked my future, a blank canvas that I saw before me, and stirred within me overwhelming doubts and questions from the mundane and practical to the personal. Where will we live? Is this right? What will I do? Who will I rely on? Where will Conor go to preschool?

One afternoon, as I took a break from packing to catch-up on emails, I got an overwhelming sense to check out the university parish in the town where we would be moving. I had been working in campus ministry for six years to date, but for a variety of reasons thought I would likely take a break from ministry work when we moved, at least until we all got settled. However, *the Spirit whispered* and I found myself emailing the staff at the university parish, attaching my resume and offering to assist however I might be helpful. As I pushed send, I laughed at my foggy desires and all this stressful situation was doing to my brain.

However, within two days I received an email from the pastor stating the following:

> *"Thank you Kelly for your recent email and resume. Your timing is interesting as a current campus ministry position has only recently become vacant and with all of the activities of the end of the year I have not had a chance to post a position description yet. You look like an interesting candidate. Can we speak soon?"*

A phone conversation led to an invitation to interview. Before I knew it, I was flying back to Michigan, toured around the parish and community and received an offer to join the campus ministry staff. It was too good to be true. It seemed that the doors were just opening, with little standing in the way, and I experienced a quiet peace within—despite the chaos and stress that flurried around me.

As I unwrapped my framed pictures and hung them on my wall in my new office, I recognized the Spirit whispers, even in Michigan.

The Spirit Whispered: You can go. It is time. Trust in me.

Prayer: Divine Spirit, you whisper through the flurried and foggy times of our lives. Thank you for meeting me where I am and breaking through my insecurities, pride and desire to control. Grant me the wisdom and courage to identify and accept your invitations, luminous beacon and unfailing guide.

Kelly Dunlop
Campus Minister at U of M
Ann Arbor, MI

"*Believe in yourself
and all that you are.
Know that there is
something inside you
that is greater than any obstacle.*"

Christian D. Larson

Whisper Fifty-Six: Have Peace, I Will Not Let You Fall

My daughter had been diagnosed with Cystic Fibrosis at four months old, and they told me she would not live past nine months. I needed to be with her because she was in and out of the hospital so much. That meant I kept taking time off from work which resulted in me losing my job. She continued to be in and out of the hospital through her teens.

One Friday morning, my daughter and I sat at the kitchen table. I was trying to figure out how to pay seven bills. I was divorced, working part-time, and struggling to make ends meet. I was alone, afraid, broke and tired. I needed help. I decided to drive three hours to my parents' home for the weekend. I knew if we went to them they would feed us and fill my car with gas.

All weekend I prayed for a miracle, but none came. A voice whispered to me, "Have peace. I will not let you fall."

On the drive back home, my daughter slept. I pleaded with God for his help. I remember crying out loud saying, "I am falling. I need $1,500 by tomorrow morning."

The ride home in the car went by quickly. I woke up my daughter, and we gathered the mail from the weekend, unpacked the car and prepared for bed.

I counted the hours I had left before I faced my debtors. I had just eight hours left. With tears in my eyes, I opened my mail.

In the stack of mail was a letter from my grandfather. He was a widower of seven years, living some distance away. My grandfather wrote, "Debi, your grandma came to me last night in a dream. She told me you were in trouble and I should send this to you!" In the envelope was a check for $1,500 with the note, "With love! Grampa."

God had heard my plea and had answered my prayers, but this was only the beginning. Not only did my daughter survive her childhood with Cystic Fibrosis but has lived past her teen years and is now thirty-four, married and has two daughters.

As you can see God has continued to work in our lives. I believe God will always be there for us. My daughter's goal is to work with the local hospital and share her story. She wants to give hope to others who have Cystic Fibrosis.

The Spirit Whispered: I want you to trust in me and be at peace. I am always here for you. I am happy to see your deep faith.

Prayer: Divine Spirit, you know the desire of my heart and what I have been going through. Your love and compassion means the world to me. I will continue to trust that you will see me through difficult and tough times.

Debbie Trail
Professional Speaker- Stephen Covey
Logan, UT

Whisper Fifty-Seven: Letting Go Is Gift

Everyone talks about how they "just knew he/she was the one" as they are getting married, but nobody talks about how "they just knew" that same person was right when they are breaking up. Brad and I were breaking up after eight years of friendship and three and a half years of being in a relationship. We had been long distance, proximate, and long distance again. The ins and outs that led us to this point would be a book in itself. We came to a point of no return—commit or leave. There was no more stay and wait. That had been done. We took a month long break to reevaluate, seek counsel, and come back together with a clearer answer and direction as to which way we would go.

When Brad and I connected again a month later, he tried to re-schedule our meeting. I already had that sinking feeling. No. The short answer to that request to push our meeting back was, no. Then, it came to the surface—in our month apart he had done nothing. Nothing. My options within this relationship were becoming rapidly limited. I could have continued to let him date me—forever, or I could accept what we needed to do. Writing this out it sounds like the decision was so clear, but in the moment it was not. Nothing made sense about having to accept that the person I loved for eight years, who loved me and promised me marriage the past three and a half years still was not ready to commnit.. I had to come to terms with the fact that this was NOTHING that was a result of what I did or did not do. I prayed, I supported, I loved, I communicated, I gave space and time and if it was going to work, it would have—even though nothing about it made sense. It was not how either of us would have planned it, but that decision to break up was reached over the phone.

He came to my apartment a day later and brought me the things I had left at his place. We cried, but it wasn't the kind of desperate cry. When I looked at him that day, I no longer saw the face of the man who would be my husband, and when I looked at his hands, I no longer saw the hands that would hold our babies. I looked at him and I saw him for what he was—a man who was broken and trying so hard to give me something he knew I wanted, but finally couldn't do it. That final goodbye was equal parts sad and beautiful. The beautiful part was grace, there is no other explanation to be given.

The following months were marked with grieving and propelling myself forward in a healing journey. Friends sent me words of wisdom to hold onto, and other times the Holy Spirit just did the talking. In a moment that I will call a "Facebook sneak attack," I found myself face to face with a new photo of Brad in Chicago, surrounded by his buddies that had been tagged by one of our mutual friends. It was like a punch in the gut and the heart. Not three posts down, a college retreat acquaintance of mine had posted something that was meant for me at that exact moment. It read:

Dear one,
When God asks you to let go of something, it's time to let it go. Once that request is made of you, the anointing lifts for you to have it and it will no longer be a source of blessing in your life.
It's ok. It's time. Can you feel it? Dare to trust his good, beautiful heart toward you. Open your white-knuckle grip and let God take out of your life what he needs to, so that he can bring into your life what he needs to next.

Wow! What an incredible gift reading those words were at that exact moment. Another gift came in the form of my counselor's words to me. I was grieving with him and telling him that, "Even though Brad and I have not spoken, I know that he is grieving this loss too because just like there is a Brad-shaped hole in my heart, I know there is an Andrea-shaped hole in his." Chip smiled kindly and said, "That's a really interesting way to look at it because you do realize that your Brad-shaped hole is actually bigger than Brad himself." He was exactly right. Brad was only part of the hole. The loss in its entirety was my hopes, dreams, and future that were wrapped up in him.

Following the breakup, I spent a great deal of time unpacking my dreams and handing them over to the author of those desires.

Some days I did it well and with grace. Other days I was convinced my heart had been broken open in a way it would never recover. God showed up in my life in the faces of my friends, family, and coworkers who taught me something about what it is to be a friend in the darkest of night. Sometimes it was a simple text, a well-timed phone call, an email, a little package of love, an invitation to dinner, or a hug that kept me going. Each person offered me the stitches I needed to piece my heart back together. They gave me the momentum to continue taking one step and then one more; one breath, and then another.

Today I stand on the other side of the hard, slow, self-reflective work of grieving and healing—though it is quite an ongoing process to commit to. A new beginning in my life came exactly a year to the date when my last relationship started falling apart. I prayed shamelessly (because God says to ask, right?) "God, if it's possible, can I just go on a date with my future husband on the anniversary of Brad's and my breakup?" I made sure God knew I was being pretty flexible and reasonable here since that really was giving him a month's time to work with, but your will be done, of course. A year and two days after Brad and I decided to take a break, Greg and I met.

With Greg, things are different—it's easy. He looks at me, kisses my forehead, and says, "I am just the luckiest guy," and I look at him and think the exact same thing, but the other way around. He is kind and loving and has a magnetic personality that he knows no-thing about. He's also not a stranger to heartbreak, which I am convinced only allows someone to love more. It doesn't make sense, but I've found it to be true for myself too. The way I am able to love him is different—deeper than I could have before Brad. It wasn't long before Greg wanted to introduce me to the people in his world. A year to date from the emotional breakup with Brad, I sat in front of Greg's parents, meeting them for the first time at dinner, soaking in the grace that got us here, heart brimming with gratitude.

I don't know where this path is leading, but I do know the reality is that living in God's story for us means trusting beyond what our

207

eyes can see. It means living in the tension and the unknown, but trusting that God is found in this place and will not leave us there. It's trusting that God authors only stories of great love and glory and God asking you to let go is also a gift, though it may seem like the most unfathomable loss to the untrained eye.

The Spirit Whispered: It's time to let go.

Prayer: Divine Spirit, give me the grace and the strength to let go of things it is time to release. Give me the space to grieve, heal, and trust that you wouldn't ask me to let go of something without replacing it with something even better. Allow me to trust my heart in your healing hands and be patient with your slow, brilliant, beautiful work.

Andrea Hanley
Child Life Specialist
Ann Arbor, MI

Whisper Fifty-Eight: My Healing Hug

Last summer I was going through a rough time and felt lost and alone. One day, I felt especially disconnected. I wasn't able to connect on the phone or in person with any of my friends or relatives. I desperately needed someone to talk to and connect with. One of my closest friends gives the most loving bear hugs and I just really wanted to talk to her and have her give me one of those hugs. I was driving around town and found myself driving by my home parish. I decided to go inside and pray. I always felt at peace in the Eucharistic Chapel. Once inside, realizing I was alone, I knelt down, put my head down and let it all out. I said to God all the things I wanted to say to my friends and family but couldn't. I told God about my true feelings, my worries, and my concerns. After shedding lots of tears, I felt a sense of peace. I felt like I just spent time with a dear and precious friend.

I continued to pray, and then spent some time in silence listening. Finally, I said to God, "I know you're here. I know you're with me and I am so thankful for that. I could still really use a hug. I wish you could give me a hug.'"

Moments later, I felt a tap on my arm. I looked up to see the face of a woman I had never seen before. She said to me "I don't know why, but God wants you to have this." She gave me a flower and a hug. That was the best hug I have ever received.

God answered my prayer. That day the Spirit knew I needed a very concrete answer to my prayers. This whisper made me more aware of all the ways the Spirit is with me. The Spirit continues to work in my life, and I feel God's presence sometimes through strangers but especially through my best friend.

The Spirit Whispered: I am here. I am always with you. I will find a way to give you what you need.

Prayer: Divine Spirit, thank you for your presence both on that day and every day. Thank you for being there and answering my prayers in just the way I needed them. Help me to be more aware of your presence in my daily life.

Claudia Molter
Teacher
Plymouth, MI

Whisper Fifty-Nine: I'll Never Give Up and Never Lose Hope!

I grew up in Greenville, South Carolina. I came from a typical Catholic family with five children. My dad traveled a lot with his work, and my mom was a stay at home mom. As a large family, it seemed like everyone wanted our parents' attention. Being the youngest, I felt invisible.

I went to college at Chapel Hill in North Carolina. While there, I joined a sorority. I wanted to fit in, and felt I had to be thin to be accepted. I became obsessed about my weight, which has continued to be a problem off and on for twenty-six years.

My parents became concerned about me when they heard about Karen Carpenter's death. It was 1983, I was 19 and weighed only 68 pounds. I was 12 pounds lighter than Karen Carpenter. Eating disorders and anorexia nervosa hit the news because of her death. At that time, however, the problem was not yet fully understood by the medical field.

My parents were very concerned when they came to visit me and saw how thin I had become. They placed me in a medical center mental health unit for a year. I had intense therapy. I had gained 40 pounds and weighed 107 pounds by the time I left. That didn't last long.

My parents were becoming more and more concerned about me. A family friend told them about a woman in Ohio who had a PhD in nutrition. My parents immediately put me on a plane to Ohio.

The woman there was a little unconventional but wanted to help me. She stripped me and took pictures, so I could see how I really looked. I desperately really wanted help and prayed this program would work. I was a good patient and did pretty well with her program. After I left, I had to call her every night at 6:00 and tell her what I ate and how I felt. Her methods worked for a while but then I would start falling backwards, even though I always wanted to get better.

In 2008, I ran for three hours every morning before dawn. I wasn't eating much and wasn't sleeping very well either. Someone gave me the book, "Gaining: The Truth about Life after Eating Disorders," by Aimee Liu. This book changed my life. I was so deeply affected by what she said in her book that I wrote to her. I never dreamed that she would write back to me. I discovered that we had so much in common that we soon became dear friends.

Randy and I asked Aimee Liu to come to Ann Arbor to speak at the University to all those who suffer from this eating disorder. I knew her words could help so many, just as they helped me.

The media interviewed me for an article in the newspaper. I was not prepared for the outpouring of phone calls, letters and emails. I didn't realize how many people were suffering and desperate for this type of information and help. Aimee shared her story with the audience. It was a powerful message that touched so many who had come to the talk.

I became involved with the Academy for Eating Disorders in the Chicago area and finally found a therapist who understood me and more importantly, recovery. I was ready to embark on a new treatment plan, and for the first time I began to really feel I could conquer my disease.

In 2011, my family moved to Charleston, South Carolina. I immediately became involved in the community. I soon realized there was a lack of resources available to treat children and adolescents who were dealing with eating disorders. I found out that local schools were trying their best to assist with the number of cases they were seeing, and families were sending their children to other states, like North Carolina, for treatment.

I spent 24 months doing personal research on the subject and was disheartened by the statistics. The S.C. Department of Mental Health states that anorexia is the third most common chronic illness among adolescents and estimates that of the 8 million Americans who suffer with an eating disorder, 95 percent of those are between the ages of 12 and 25. Further, 50 percent of girls between the ages of 11 and 13 see themselves as overweight and 80 percent of 13-year-olds have already attempted to lose weight.

When I learned that the mortality rate associated with anorexia nervosa is 12 times higher than the death rate related to all causes of death for females 15-24 years old, I was appalled.

I knew I had to do something so Randy and I donated money to fund a pediatric intensive outpatient center at Medical University of South Carolina,[MUSC] and with the help of Charles Darby Jr., M.D., professor emeritus and executive director of the Center for Child Advocacy, $1 million has been raised.

Randy and I have committed our time and resources to help the MUSC Department of Pediatrics recruit a first class team of specialists to form a center of excellence in eating disorders, and we are committed to researching the causes, treatments and methods of prevention.

I am completely committed to this project. Anorexia robbed me of so many important moments throughout my life. My goal now is to help others understand this illness and by completing my M.S. in psychology I hope to work directly with those who need help the most.

I am a survivor and I am healthy. I talk to my therapist in Ann Arbor once a week to keep me focused and strong. For nearly thirty years I lived a nightmare, but now I live my dreams with my devoted husband, Randy and our four beautiful children. The love and support of my family keeps me going and helps me want to take care of myself. I love them very much.

The Spirit Whispered: Don't give up. I will help you through this. Trust in me.

Prayer: Divine Spirit, I need your strength and guidance to fight this. I know I can do anything with your help.

Donna Friedman
Graduate Student at Nova Southern University
Mt. Pleasant, SC

Whisper Sixty: Growing up in Faith, Age and Wisdom

I did not like God very much when I was a young adult. I grew up in the so-called "perfect Catholic family" when, in the 1950, we memorized the seven this and the twelve that and knew all the minutiae of Catholic doctrine. The emphasis was on a God who wanted us to be perfect, avoid all temptations of sin (way before we even knew what that meant) and above all, we were never to bring shame or embarrassment to our parents or, God forbid, give scandal to the non-Catholic world that surrounded us. Giving scandal was much worse than any injustice in our moral sanctuary.

In my teens I was extremely impressed by the poem, "The Hound of Heaven" by Francis Thompson (1857-1908). We must have studied it in our Catholic high school before Vatican II when Catholics were often more likely to read mystical poetry than the Sacred Scriptures. To this day I can recite lines from the poem. Frankly, I was scared to death of God. I fully thought God would "hound" me all my days if I did not do exactly everything perfectly the way he wanted it done. I felt like I would disappear if I let God into my life.

I didn't grow up in my faith and knowledge about God until I was almost thirty. I was working at a small college and December was an extremely busy month with grading papers and preparing for the next semester. After Christmas with my family, I made a private retreat at a cloistered convent in Detroit where the senior girls in my high school had made a retreat. I was very tired and I had a serious cold. My retreat director realized immediately that I needed to sleep for a few days before I paid attention to my spiritual life. One night my fever broke and I was awake for hours crying about my life and being angry at God for hounding me "down the days and nights."

So many changes were occurring in the world and the church during the late 60s early 70s including Vatican II, the Civil Rights movement, the Vietnam War and the women's movement. The Hippies were spreading their messages of peace and love, the Beatles were singing "love is all there is" and parents and children were fighting over issues like long hair. It was a very challenging time for all long-established institutions including our churches and families. Psychologists were stressing self-esteem. For the first time it seems I really heard about the greatest Commandment: "You shall love the Lord thy God and your neighbor as yourself." I was astounded. "There are these three: faith, hope and love and the greatest of these is love." "God is love." The messages were coming from every side.

A popular poster of the day showed a small child with a message: "God made me and God doesn't make junk." That poster was the Spirit whispering to me during this upheaval in my life.

I woke up one night in the middle of my retreat with an over-whelming conviction that a loving God had created me, and that I was not being true to that all loving God if I did not love myself. I had been created by a God of life who came to this earth that we may have life. I became convinced that God was not some kind of merciless tyrant who would create a person and then condemn that person as worthless junk, undeserving of love. The words of St. Paul played over and over in my head. "When I was a child, I thought as a child." I knew right there that I had to give up all my childish, inaccurate ideas of God. It felt like my life depended on having a new image of God, a new relationship with God. I also had to embrace a new image of myself. I grew up into an adult human being that night and I became a grown-up adult Christian. I had to take responsibility for my life. That was God's will for me and not trying to become a perfect, guilt-ridden, obsessive person who thought she was being hounded by God.

I can honestly say that since that night I have had an image of God that makes me feel happy, safe and comforted. I love to repeat certain psalms and hymns over and over to myself, "The Lord is my rock and my salvation. Of whom shall I be afraid? The Lord is my light." No matter what has happened to me or what craziness I experience in this world I truly believe in a God who loves me, who is my rock, my light and my salvation. I want to love and serve that God. "All will be well."

The Spirit Whispered: God doesn't make junk. God loves you as if you were the only person he created.

Prayer: Divine Spirit, thank you for my life, for faith, hope and love. Help me to grow stronger every day in these beliefs. You continue to sustain me through all the challenges of old age as you have through all my years. I am very grateful and I want to sing your praises all my days. I know you are with me as my rock, my light and my salvation. You are the Way, the Truth and the Life. I believe.

Margaret Beahan, Retired
Michigan Department of Education
Lansing, MI

―――――― • ――――――

"Creator Spirit whispers in us,
'Rise Up! Make your journey!
Bring to birth the dream
I have planted in your soul.'"

Author Unknown

―――――― • ――――――

Whisper Sixty-One: The Working of the Spirit

This fall our son, Eddie, will enter Michigan State University as part of the freshman class of 2014. This is significant to our family in many ways. Eddie is our firstborn, and although tens of millions of people across the globe will do the same thing this fall, we imagine that watching him leave our home will be a moment filled with great pride as well as sadness. In the state of Michigan, collegiate loyalties are shaped early in one's life and although there are some exceptions, most people find themselves aligned with either the University of Michigan (U of M) in Ann Arbor, or Michigan State University (MSU) in East Lansing. The rivalry revolves mostly around two sports teams. While it is a relatively friendly rivalry, it is indeed spirited. There are households each football season and each basketball season that consider themselves a 'house divided.' I mention all of this because I have always been affiliated, either simply in my thoughts, or more formally during my clinical training, with U of M, but I never imagined that this playful rivalry would ever become part of a message, a whisper, from God.

Twenty-five years ago I was searching; searching for God, stability, and joy. I showed up for Mass occasionally but not often at St. Thomas More Student Parish in Kalamazoo, where I was a student at Western Michigan University (WMU). I had heard about a student retreat that would be taking place. I can't say that I recall the details of how I decided to attend, but I did, and that single weekend changed the course of my life forever. Before I proceed, it's important for me to say that in my current job, in addition to teaching on the faculty at WMU, I also conduct research, and speaking (or even thinking) in grandiose ways such as "...that single weekend changed the course of my life forever" is not part of the typically conservative frame of mind associated with my work and daily experience. The fact remains, however, that the brief period of time on retreat allowed me the quiet I needed to better hear God's whispers and also brought his megaphone into my life, Sr. Dorothy Ederer.

Sr. Dorothy wasn't loud but she was clear. Her relationship with Jesus was real and unambiguous, and she showed me how mine could be also. I was, and am, a percussionist and Sr. Dorothy invited me to bring my drums to Mass and play as part of the music ministry.

I remember saying to her, "I'm finally trying to get closer to God and more involved in the church and you're going to get me thrown out!" She, and God, assured me that I should just play the drums, be myself, and everything would be okay. And that was it. That was the initial spark, the first whisper, the first call from God where I responded with a tentative but willing 'yes'; that was the first step on what has become a two and a half decade journey. I played at Mass from that point forward and almost every week the congregation applauded after the closing song and some parishioners stopped by to share how God had spoken to them through the music during Mass. Some of these people were permanent residents but many were other 18-25 year old college students.

After graduating from college, I moved to New York, just outside of New York City. It wasn't long after that Sr. Dorothy moved to upstate New York to pursue her work with Fr. Joe Girzone and the Joshua Foundation. My friends from Michigan and St. Thomas More met upstate every summer for years to provide music for the Joshua retreats led by Fr. Joe and Sr. Dorothy. Each person had their own message, their own whisper if you will, from God and I kept listening.

A number of years later, I, along with my wife Karen, and our 2-year-old son, moved to Fort Collins, Colorado for graduate school, and I felt deeply disconnected from my Joshua family. Then one Christmas, during the two years in Colorado, my wife surprised me with a plane ticket to fly back to New York in the summer so I could participate in the Joshua retreat. I didn't fully realize it until then, but Karen fully recognized that my relationship with Jesus was always deepened during those retreats. She could hear God's whispers better than I, and often passed on his messages through her love.

Not long after graduating and moving back to Kalamazoo, I happened to be in Colorado for work. For reasons I do not recall, I called Fr. Joe who asked me if I had plans that night. When I said that I didn't, he made a few phone calls and the next thing I knew, I was in Denver attending the premier of the cinematic release of the movie, *Joshua,* based on Fr. Joe's first book of the same title. Because Fr. Joe couldn't be there, he asked me to serve as his 'eyes and ears' and to let him know how closely the final version of the movie corresponded with his book. I remember wondering if my being there was a simple fortuitous coincidence or if somehow it was all part of God's larger plan.

It has been 14 years since we moved back to Kalamazoo as a family. Now, in addition to our son, Eddie, we also have a 13-year old daughter, Heather. Heather has been clear that she will miss her brother terribly when he leaves for school. Do you want to know what makes her feel better and quiets our hearts, as well? Sr. Dorothy, the same person who welcomed me more fully into a relationship with Jesus twenty-five years and three relocations ago, is now the Director of Campus Ministry at the Catholic student parish at Michigan State University. She'll be waiting for my son when he gets there.

The Spirit Whispered: I never leave. I am always here. Trust me.

Prayer: Divine Spirit, please forgive my unending doubts, thank you for your constant presence, and help me to be an instrument of peace and healing for all your people.

Edward A. Roth
Professor of Music Therapy
Kalamazoo, MI

"*Pay attention to the whispers, the nudges, the urgings. Your soul is begging, your life is waiting.*"

Author Unknown

Index of Citations

CPSIA information can be obtained
at www.ICGtesting.com
Printed in the USA
LVOW04s2049101115

461889LV00020B/1142/P

9 781623 110277